COME YOU HERE, BOY!

COME YOU HERE, BOY!

Alan Bloom

ISIS
LARGE PRINT
Oxford, England

First published in Great Britain 1995
by Aidan Ellis Publishing

Published in Large Print 1995 by ISIS Publishing Ltd,
7 Centremead, Osney Mead, Oxford OX2 0ES,
by arrangement with Aidan Ellis

British Library Cataloguing in Publication Data
Bloom, Alan
    Come You Here, Boy!
    I. Title
    635.092

ISBN 1-85695-129-4

Printed and bound by Hartnolls Ltd, Bodmin, Cornwall

CONTENTS

Incentives

Until fairly recent years, scarcely any of the visiting public recognised me. To the vast majority, on the then twice-weekly openings, the elderly man driving the little steam engine taking people round on its two and a half mile track was one of the staff. I dodged some of the questions, such as who did the place belong to? Was I a retired railway driver? Being dressed for the part and often grubby from engine smoke, such questions were natural, but I preferred not to let out that I was responsible for both the Steam Museum and the five-acre garden adjoining.

Then came television and I finally gave way by allowing a small photo of myself in the guide book. I could no longer pretend, and now each time my train comes back to the station platform there are cameras aimed at me and usually someone wishing to speak to me. If I'm engrossed in such duties as attending to the engine's needs — fire, water and oil — then they have to wait, especially if I'm asked to sign a guide book, which is the most usual request. But it's those who come to thank me or to say how much they have enjoyed their visit who please and touch me most, prompting a feeling of warmth towards them.

One hot August afternoon, within a short space of time, two men came up to express themselves in a way which gave me such food for thought that I felt urged to write a book. The first was a portly, well-spoken, middle-aged man who had just taken a ride on my train.

"Do you ever reflect," he asked rather pompously, "on the sheer wealth you have created here? I don't mean entirely in money terms, though you must be a millionaire, I'd imagine. What I envy you is being able to see on all sides so much that you own of interest and value. Surely you must be very proud of your achievements?"

As usual, when I'm assumed to be the owner I shrink inside, wanting to deny ownership, having given away practically all my assets; some to the Steam Museum Trust and the rest to my family — retaining only one per cent of the shares in Blooms Nurseries Ltd. The man's remarks had put me on edge and as briefly as possible I explained my position.

"But you don't have to feel any the less proud do you? It's still your personal creation and you can't deny that. I know what I'd feel if I were in your shoes — and that's why I envy you."

There was neither a case nor the time to extend the argument, so I closed it by smiling some appreciation, adding that I saw no cause for pride when so aware of how much more remained to be done. His face wore a puzzled look as he gave way to someone else who edged in for me to sign a guide book. But the man's attitude continued to bother me somehow for a while, for it was almost aggressive as well as being wide of the mark. I didn't feel proud in the way he meant it. I never have nor ever wish to, because of the enjoyment I derived over the years in making the place what it has become. If indeed it can be seen as creative on my part, I am probably the only one aware of its sublimatory content.

The next encounter to cause some thoughts at variance with the pleasant routine of engine driving occurred on that same afternoon as I was oiling the bearings of *Bronwllyd*. Bent low, a man's voice came from behind. His speech was low and somewhat confidential. "I hope you don't mind," he said, "but ever since I saw you on that TV programme a few weeks back, I can't get out of my mind something you said — near the end it was."

He stood back to allow me to replace the oil can on the footplate and gave me half a smile as I wiped my fingers on a rag.

"What was that?" I asked, trying to put him at his ease with a smile.

He too was of middle age and middle class by his speech, which was inclined to be deferential. He then explained that he'd seen the BBC Look Stranger programme on me on what happened to be its third showing in about four years, and my concluding remarks had made him ponder deeply.

"Geoff Hamilton asked if you were a happy man. You didn't answer straight away, yes or no. You just smiled like and then said you still enjoyed working and had a lot to be thankful for, but admitted you'd made some blunders. And then you said — and this is what got me — that you hadn't been punished as you might have been and maybe deserved to be for some of them. And that made me think, it did, for a man in your position to say such a thing."

Whether or not he wished to explain why my remarks

had affected him so much I could not tell, but his general attitude, both confidential and deferential, affected me too. I would not have expected him to ask what kind of blunders I'd made or why I deserved punishment for them, but there was no doubt of his sincerity. Nor was there time, because from behind came the shrill whistle to take the train now loaded with people. As I stood up to pip the engine's whistle and nudge open the regulator, the man held out his hand for me to shake.

It needed full concentration when hauling the five coach train carrying up to 100 people on a down gradient, with lots of pedestrians around. The notice of 3 m.p.h. is needful on that stretch of track, and it was not until we reached the level of the valley bottom that my thoughts went back to the stranger who had based his concern on what I'd said rather glibly for the TV interview. Not that in the pensive spells which often occur when working alone with plants I avoid reminding myself of what I referred to as blunders. Yet blunders most of them were, at least in my own considered estimation. I am in no position to sit in impartial judgment upon my past to settle beyond further dispute what were mistakes and what were misdeeds. Some linger to cause me shameful regret, but I have learned that remorse and abject feelings of guilt are as harmful as they are negative. Life has to be lived positively or it is not worth living.

Life, rather than Christian doctrines, has taught me that a vital factor in our human inheritance is that we all possess the capacity for both good and evil. And in living positively we are no less — and maybe more — likely to veer off the straight and narrow way into wrongdoing.

The old statement that the way to hell is paved with good intentions holds considerable truth for me too, for with hindsight I can now see clearly some of the false notions which, to say the least, caused hurt to others. It's all very well to lump my misdeeds under the heading of blunders. Just because I didn't stop to think hard enough is no excuse. Nor is there any mitigation in confessing that I never set out to hurt anyone while convincing myself that what I wanted to do appeared at the time to be the right thing. On such occasions, conscience took a back seat as my imagination, ambition and enthusiasm took control, spurring me into positive action.

These admissions are in a sense by the way, but are made so as to clear the way for some explanation on the theme of punishment. It has been said of me that I'm by nature a glutton for punishment, but this was with reference to my past propensity for tackling zestfully projects involving hard labour and anxiety — as a facet of positivity in action. But oddly, perhaps the lifelong susceptibility to incurring stress and punishment has been quite distinct from any retribution for my misdeeds through lacking sensitivity towards other people's interests or feelings. Punishment came not from outside but from within myself for lack of self-knowledge, unable or failing to come to terms with my own basic, inborn nature. Inner conflict raged on and off for almost my whole life, its pricks and bruisings ceasing only when I became engrossed or obsessed in some venture, or when up against some extraneous problem.

It was not until I reached the age of seventy that at

last I began to know and accept myself as I was; and so peace replaced conflict gradually, little by little. It was this blessed peace which enabled me to see how fortunate I have been over the years in so many ways. The memories of mental perplexity and anguish evaporated to such an extent as to appear to wipe my slate clean, as if no punishment had ever been made. Not that at times of distress I ever saw this as punishment in itself, but only as a very personal morass into which I was so often prone to fall. There were times when both my brain and body seized up, as it were, like a log jam. I'd feel a slackness beyond my will, and I had to give in by slinking away out of sight, avoiding contact with others whenever possible, becoming sleepy and listless. Those lapses were well spaced and lasted two or three days at most, and then quite suddenly lifted and I would find myself again with renewed strength and resolve. The ups had begun to outnumber the downs.

The process of self discovery was slow but came together rather like the pieces of a jigsaw puzzle, one by one, till at last the pattern became ever more apparent. I'd consulted psychiatrists during my middle years but none had come up with a satisfactory answer. I had studied the Bible and books on religion and theology, but none had offered either consolation or guidance which I could follow. But from my mid-sixties onwards other books on human nature afforded flashes of recognition applicable to my problem, so that pieced together they began to make sense. Instead of fears that I might be going round the bend, as was the case when I was sixty-three, the way ahead to self discovery straightened out and began to put the past into perspective. The possibility and even probability that my particular eccentricity was of genetic origin was intriguing, more so than its being due to some hormone imbalance at a natal stage. So it was that mental and emotional turmoil gave way so late in life to a grateful sense of relief, with a measure of uncomplacent serenity. Robust health, coupled with ample zest to make the best possible use of what time remains for me, goes well beyond what the first of those two men saw as my achievements. As for the second one, I can but say that the thought of not being adequately punished for past blunders does not weigh heavily. With plans in mind for the future it would be wise not to anticipate retribution still to come upon me. It will be far better to use what wisdom I may have gained from past errors and apply it also in writing this book. Some incentive to write it came from a third man not long after the other encounters. An ex-British Rail driver with a liking for steam had come regularly for many years as a volunteer on Open Days. In asking for a copy of one of my more recent books, A Plantsman's Perspective, he gave me a quizzical smile. "I'm not all that interested in plants," he admitted, "but someone who'd read it told me you let yourself go in parts of it. That's why I want to read it, because I'd dearly love to know what makes you tick."

What follows in this book should do just that for Bill and for whoever else cares to read it.

Growing Pains and Pleasures

Many years later my parents told me that I was not expected to survive babyhood. At four months my weight had fallen from ten pounds at birth to seven pounds because no food had been found that I could digest. Dr Ellis came again on a Sunday morning in March 1907 because I'd gone into a coma. He turned the coverlet back and tapped my distended belly. "Oh dear," he said. "Poor little beggar, he'll never open his eyes again — he's drum-bellied." But a few hours later my eyes did re-open. It so happened that my parents had enticed down yet another brand of baby food early that morning — Allenburys — and at last I'd responded. Apart from occasional bilious attacks thereafter, my physical growth progressed normally.

This episode has no bearing on what follows, nor can I imagine being aware for the next two or three years that I was of the male sex. In those days babies and toddlers were dressed with few distinctions regarding sex. This practice was common to all classes and might well have been a hangover from Victorian times or even earlier. I have an old family photograph which shows me in what appears to be a frock at about three years of age, and one of my earliest memories is of having my first hair cut. Another, even earlier memory, probably before my fourth birthday, is equally vivid and this had, I imagine, a profound bearing in my future life. Circumstantial evidence rather than a clear awareness, potent enough to be imprinted on my earliest memory, points strongly to the wish to have been a girl.

I think this emerged before I was fully aware that I was in fact a boy. I doubt very much if I could have kept the wish a secret from my mother, or my sister, three years older than me. She told me years later that she, in fact, wished I'd been a girl, and took an active dislike to me when any boyishness became apparent. And I can imagine that at three years old I was, in those circumstances, no more sex conscious than to assume that the difference was merely a matter of dress and hair length. At any rate it's a pretty safe assumption that my mother knew of my preference. She may well have been perplexed as to how best to deal with it, but more likely believed it was something I would soon lose or grow out of with no regrets. As a very practical, down-to-earth person, it would not have occurred to her even to ask why I wanted to be a girl, but she would see any such wish as superficial, a passing whim on my part. I might not even have confided my wish, because not only was she rather undemonstrative in her affections, but she had already unthinkingly deceived me.

My father was an early riser with a passion for growing things, and he would often spend an hour or two in his garden or greenhouse before opening his general village shop. Mother preferred to lie in a while, for her work scarcely ceased till bed time. I was still in a cot in the parental bedroom and woke asking for a drink of water whilst mother was dozing alone in the double bed. She told me I could join her. "And if you lie still on your back and keep your mouth open some drops of water may come from the ceiling." I believed her until, after what seemed a long time, I became even more conscious of thirst. Mother finally said it was time to get dressed and then I'd get my drink, as if it were a joke to say water would drop from the ceiling — a joke I could not appreciate.

I fancy the next and more vital episode was also thought of as a joke. It was shared by her younger, unmarried sister. Aunt Etty was a nurse and had come to stay for a holiday, and she too had a sense of humour which included a special relish for practical jokes. I think it likely that the telling to Aunt Etty of my wish to be a girl coincided with the period of childhood when boys should shed any remaining evidence of sharing what they wore with girls. It could be that I had already been put into knickers, as knee-length trousers were then called. But it could also well be that I still believed that somehow clothing was a determining factor. In any case, the wish to be or to have been born a girl was still alive.

"And so you shall," either or both might well have declared. I was in Mother's bedroom at the time and don't remember any others being around. My younger brother George might have been with Kathleen and Eric downstairs. Memory holds on only to outstanding essential details of what was sharply defined. I was told to undress in front of the long wardrobe mirror and very soon Mother came back from Kathleen's adjoining bedroom with an armful of her outgrown clothes, underwear and all. Dumb with suppressed joy, excitement and wonder, both women fussed over the dressing. My still long hair was carefully brushed and if I cannot be sure that it was topped by a bow of ribbon, more likely than not it was.

"What a pretty girl you are! Turn round, let's see you from behind and then you can look at yourself in the mirror." In a daze, unable to say what I felt, not daring to question the future in the magic of the present, I do not remember what I did or what Mother and Aunt Etty said or did after their first appraisal. My shirt, vest, knickerbockers and socks were on the bed. My mind was in such a state that, if I had been told I would never have to wear them again and that I was now a real girl, I would have believed it with the utmost contentment. I might have pranced around whilst Mother and Aunt Etty chatted about things which did not concern me. I might have wished or even asked if I could go downstairs and show myself to my brothers and sister, to the servant in the kitchen or to those in the shop, but none of these have a place in my memory. And then, after I don't know how long, came the end, startling like the sudden, unexpected cracking of a whip, or like falling off a high wall on to hard ground.

"Time to change back into your proper clothes! And from now on, you must be a real boy and never again wear girls' clothes. We only dressed you up for a bit of fun and now it's all over. You must surely *want* to be a big strong boy, don't you? And do all sorts of things girls can't do?"

Such remarks were no doubt made, but whatever the wording the message was as stark and clear as it was devastating to me. I doubt if I burst into a fit of tears or made any kind of protest. I might have been more aware of my true sex than is indicated by the way I have described the episode. But it was real and so was its shattering effect on me. It was perhaps the first occasion in my life when I found it easier to carry secret thoughts and longings and to indulge in fantasies by way of relief. But another blow came soon afterwards, which had a hardening effect on me in the need to keep certain thoughts as secrets.

Having turned four I was told it was time I went to school. The choice could only be the smaller of the two village schools since it belonged to the Church. Father was persuaded, I guess, to take me on the front carrier of his bike and not to tell me in advance where he was going. Probably by pre-arrangement, in view of my reluctance, the morning session had begun. Taking me by the hand he led me to the infants' door and I was taken over by the teacher and the door closed behind me. But I took fright at what I saw — lots of children and a huge contraption which I learned later was the heating stove. I broke free and caught up with Father who earned my gratitude when he agreed that after all I was a bit too young.

At about the same time Mother invited me to go with her by train to St Ives. It was the nearest market town only one station away. She had some shopping to do but went first to one which sold toys. It was next door to a barber's saloon and I was not to know there was a connecting inner door between the two.

"Now you just go in there and wait for me and I'll bring you that toy," she said after I'd been asked to stay outside looking at the window display. I did as I was told, and a man wearing an apron invited me to sit on a high chair and wait for Mother to come with my toy. He fiddled with a small white sheet and, standing behind me, put it round my shoulders. Then just as Mother appeared through the connecting door came the feel and click of scissors at the back of my neck, along with a sense of outrage as another fistful of hair was sheared off. I began to struggle, but Mother made consoling noises as she handed me the toy. I don't remember what it was, but I snatched it and threw it on the floor with despairing tears and a deep resentment at having been tricked into losing my one remaining affinity with girls.

The incident rankled as much for its deception as for its loss to me. But no longer could I hang on to any secret pretensions, and in the light of changing attitudes towards life, of having to adapt, to be realistic, the rankling ceased. But the incident itself became indelible on my mind, along with the water drops from the ceiling, and both later became a somewhat amusing grudge against Mother. It was not until long after she died over forty years later that full and true perspective came. I needed to understand myself in order to understand that she did what she believed to be right and was not to be blamed, least of all by me. She was a product of her own generation and its social mores and morals, just as I am of mine. Neither she nor any of her five brothers and two sisters were very demonstrative with their affections or feelings. Father and his two brothers and five sisters were somewhat more open, but all were conditioned by the sternly religious attitudes of their own times. There was no clear distinction between religion and the prevailing social conventions, and at a very early age the importance of both was an essential part of being nurtured. But having accepted that I was a boy and must grow up to become strong and manly, there was no ban on keeping to myself some very secret thoughts.

After the abortive attempt, I finally accepted the necessity of schooling and found the rule of boys sharing two-seater desks with a girl much to my liking. It was in fact quite comforting, and at break time I had no other inclination than to play with the girls in their part of the gravelled yard. "Ring o' Roses" and "Wallflowers" were favourite games, but after a time I was tempted to show how strong and agile I was. Inspired by their adoration of how high or far I could jump, the next exhibition was in climbing. There were no trees, but against the school wall was a rain water tub on a raised block well above ground level. After much effort I managed to stand on the wooden cover of the tub to take in the admiring looks from the pinafored girls down below. There were, after all, some distinct advantages in being a boy. But paying too little attention to my foothold, the lid suddenly tilted and down I dropped up to my chest in water, clutching the rim of the tub, scarcely able to see over the top. Several screams, probably mine included, brought the girls near, including Ruth Thoday who was in the top class. She quickly found a foothold and with strong hands under my armpits hauled me out. She lived less than a stone's throw away and with teacher's permission took me home, dried me and found clothes for me till mine were dried. The gratitude I felt for Ruth was lasting and found expression years later in letters we exchanged every few months; hers to me becoming barely legible from the effects of arthritis in old age.

This mishap marked the first stage of a switch to playing with boys of my own age. Perhaps I'd become cockily proud of my strength, which of course girls would in time disdain. Another thing was that I was learning not to cry when hurt. Becoming more aware of the advantages in being a boy seemed to emphasise the disadvantages there obviously were in being a girl. But for me, there was another cause for concern.

It must have been late in the hot summer of 1911 whilst I was still under five. Some cousins came to stay and I was told to move temporarily into Kathleen's room. Both George and I were still expected to be in bed well before seven p.m. which was a cause for much resentment. Being sent to bed even earlier was a standard form of punishment for a misdemeanour, and disobedience was often as not the cause. It wasn't fair to be sent to bed so early when we knew other children remained at play on summer evenings till eight or nine. That evening I fretted and sweated, in no mood to sleep. Whether or not there was any forethought I don't remember, but I slid out of bed and began to investigate the contents of a chest of drawers. One of them I knew must be of Kathie's outgrown clothes, including the dress I'd worn months before. The temptation became unbearable, but I dare not put it on even though both Father and Mother had already been up to say goodnight — a kiss from Father and a peck from Mother, who was always in a hurry because she was so busy. And I'd already said my prayers, "Gentle Jesu, meek and mild . . ."

Outside the light was fading by the time I decided to compromise. I dare not dress overall because there would be no escape or excuse if anyone came through that open door. So, taking off my nightshirt, I pulled on a vest that was tight over my chest and all the better for that, and a pair of cotton knickers which had a lace frill over the knee and a button at the side to fasten. The thrill was made all the nicer for those garments being so much softer in texture than my nightshirt, and as I slipped back into bed I wanted to stay awake even though I felt so much peace and contentment. Having them hidden under my nightshirt I also felt safe.

At half past six next evening, and the next, I went to bed without resentment, but when I folded the garments to place them back in the drawer on the third morning I realised that someone, sometime, would notice they'd been worn. Anxiety grew and, instead of repeating the change for the fourth time, I fretted and sweated, not from heat, but from fear. It was a fear that grew such in size and shape as to convince me that I had committed a great sin. Not only was there an accusation I could not deny except by stubborn lying which would compound my crime, but I risked incurring God's wrath too, having learned already of Judgment Day and Hell Fire for the wicked. It would be so awful. Seeing no hope of forgiveness, there remained no way out other than to carefully conceal the soiled garments underneath all the others in the drawer. In addition I must resolve never to do such a thing again and in future to be above reproach in every respect, hoping thereby to earn forgiveness on the Day of Judgment. After all, at every church service everyone said they were miserable sinners, and God didn't desire the death of sinners but required them to turn away from their wickedness and live.

In time such terrors, including nightmares which left me gasping when I woke up, were offset by periods of well-being. I can think of several older women who were especially kind to me. One was a school teacher, and two of the shop assistants as well as Maud Smith who helped in the house. Another was the elderly Mrs Leggett whose husband pumped the organ bellows in church and whose daughter Lottie had been nursemaid to George and me. And, apart from the delights of roaming the fens and meadows by day, there were times on still winter nights when before going up to bed I used to linger over the last visit to the closet. This was at the end of a path between sheds and the garden, well screened by evergreens. On the way back I often became enthralled when gazing up at the starlit sky. In the silence I thought I could hear a low musical tone which I guessed must be the stars singing to each other, though later I knew this was the tinnitus which has never left me.

The awareness of guilt took years to shake off. It also caused side effects, the most potent of which was a fear of death. The coffins we saw from the school window being carried to the church opposite and later to the graveyard were not all for old people. A few were for children who had died from diphtheria or consumption.

Perhaps I had more secrets than most other boys and was more impressionable, with a livelier imagination. The underlying urge for children in those days and in village life was to become integrated and accepted as normal. Drop outs and rebels as well as wrongdoers were rare because everyone else would tend to ostracise them. The few inhabitants who did not go to church or one of the two Nonconformist chapels were classed as degenerate outsiders.

On 1 July 1916 I first wore cassock and surplice as a choir boy and enjoyed the lusty singing. The church stood for age-old stability, and being in the choir I felt more security against the effects of an often guilty conscience because of my secret thoughts and longings. One of the latter was to wear gold rings in my earlobes as did two or three elderly men and several women. At one time I badly wanted to wear glasses because in some peculiar way I associated them with a feminine link in which a male could participate.

My path to integration and the general process of growing up was anything but smooth. Periods of being good and biddable alternated with rebellious and even rowdy moods. I alternated from being the leader of a little gang of boys lighting a fire in some hideout in the fen with Woodbines to smoke, to roaming alone sometimes to feel at one with nature. At such times I found the urge to sing irresistible with what was said to be the best treble voice in the choir. Mostly it was a hymn that came bursting out. Sometime I would lie flat in a grassy meadow, alert to any wild thing — flowers, birds and insects — and allow my fantasies to run wild too.

The World in a Village

My relationship with both Father and Mother was mostly good. I wanted to please them and every little bit of praise pleased me. Both applauded my capacity to work and habit of saving, but if Mother was all in favour of my becoming a man of business, she was sternly moralistic as well as ambitious for me.

Father worked hard but was torn between his love for flowers on the few acres he grew for market and the shop life he hated but into which he had been forced. Falling between two stools he seemed always short of capital.

His father had been stern indeed and had once sentenced him to several hours on bread and water in a locked cellar. Grandpa also objected to baby nappies being changed in his presence, but to his credit gave a tenth of his income to charity — or chapel. I fancy Father was pretty lenient with us because grandpa had considered we were unruly. The fact was that we three boys were lively and apt to be boisterous and Father was a very kindly man at heart, never shouting at us and always ready to forgive.

As a family we were no more than middle class, but in a village where there was no squire and no one more upper class than the vicar we were, along with the few other employers, a cut above the rest in some people's estimation; even if the general view was that Jack was as good as his master — a fenland trait. That Father painted pictures and Mother was an expert milliner, and both were good at acting in the annual village concert, added to the respect in which they were held for being upright, God-fearing and reliable.

I was mostly the one to be asked to take a plateful of hot dinner to an old bedridden man not far away. And I came to know almost every householder when the time came each year to hawk round bags of Father's mustard and cress, not only in Over but sometimes in the two neighbouring villages of Swavesey and Willingham. My commission was a penny in the shilling, and Father's praise for persevering salesmanship went down well. It fostered pride of achievement and my propensity for saving pennies, the latter earning the jibe of miser from my siblings.

The river Ouse, only a mile from home, had a special appeal to both George and me. We taught ourselves to swim on a pack of rushes, and in fishing graduated from gudgeon to roach and perch. In frosty winters we made slides on village roads and paths, and complained bitterly when some householder sprinkled cinders on one of our slides. Once, however, the sight of a horse which fell when hauling a load of manure as its hooves slipped on our slide was frightening, as we watched it struggle whilst pinned down by the shafts.

The notion of having fun at someone else's expense appeared to be at that time a widely accepted privilege. On later reflection this seemed to be a fenland trait, but it was not confined to people. I once saw a cat careering along the street in terror from the noise of a tin can tied to its tail. On another occasion I was invited by two young men to witness rats being drowned in the wire cage in which they had been trapped. As the most hated of all vermin it was all right to kill them, but the glee of the killers I could not share.

Horses, for all their value, were sometimes cruelly treated and by some men the whip was unsparingly used. If a heavy load failed to move out of a rut in a muddy place, the horse's struggle was intensified by fierce whipping over its flanks, as was one fallen horse I saw struggling to find its feet whilst still yoked. Worst of all was a driver who instead of a whip had a sharply pointed stick which he prodded into the animal's rectum. But there — was the use of spurs digging in from a rider's boot any less cruel?

Although falling in a ditch was my lot on several occasions, my brother George had the most embarrassing experience. He and I had wandered into the low meadows behind the vicarage, having been told that there was a pollarded willow down there with a gooseberry bush growing on it. We found it and, thinking only of ripe gooseberries, decided to climb up. Being old and pollarded it was not so much a case of climbing but clambering up. With George on my shoulder he could find a foothold and then reach down to help me up. It was exciting to sit there knowing that we could boast of having eaten gooseberries on an old willow tree. But the old limb on which George sat was rotten. It gave way as he shifted about and down he went into the ditch. The sailor suit he was wearing was no longer white and as we hurried home people laughed with such remarks as

"What you been up to, Georgie — been up a chimbly have you?"

Mother's reaction on reaching home was as expected without such humour. George was put into the tin bath which was otherwise used for our Saturday night immersion in the kitchen, with the addition of carbolic. I was given similar treatment at a later date, not for falling in a foul ditch, but because of stinking clothes. At a loose end one day I peered into Edgar Norman's yard and was invited in with, "Come you here, boy, if you want to earn a tanner (sixpence). That sty needs mucking out." I fell for the offer and set to with a will and a muck fork. It took no more than an hour, but when Edgar came to inspect he handed me four pennies with, "I don't have a tanner on me, but it didn't take you long did it, so fourpence is good enough pay." I took it with no thanks for a bad bargain and the dressing down from Mother only added to my sense of injustice.

Meanness tended to run in families. Edgar Norman was related to "Dewey" the poacher, who drove a hard bargain. His brother Jim (Moggy), who kept the Black Horse opposite our house, was adept at cadging help from boys, especially to turn the handle when grinding mangold-wortzels in the barn with the banging doors. His son Bis (Bismarck), who drove the mail cart to Cambridge every evening, once took me by surprise by offering some personal advice in a very confidential way. I was about fourteen and quite sturdy, but to be told that I needed to be stunted because I was plenty big enough already did not appeal to me at all.

"What you need to do is to smoke an ounce or two of

plug bacca in a clay pipe," he explained quite seriously. "Bein' tall is a handicap and I'm glad me father made me stop growin' when I were about your age with black plug bacca. You can easy sneak a clay pipe and the bacca outer the shop, and I'll show you how to smook it on the quiet."

There was another occasion when I brought an unwelcome smell into the house. In about 1920, when George and I had become regular hawkers every spring of not only mustard and cress but radishes and flowers to prolong the season well into May, Father decided we should try selling bloaters from door to door to extend the practice even longer. At first sales were quite good, confined as they were to bloaters and smoked haddock obtained from Cambridge by train in boxes. But as so often happened when selling far away from home, hunger was a problem and George confessed to eating some haddock whilst hawking in St Ives, uncooked though it was. I'd been given the Over and Swavesey round that year and having sold out I persuaded Father to let me buy the fish out of my savings the following year and keep all the profit. This appealed to my rising business instincts, but naturally George wanted nothing to do with it.

With just bloaters to sell at three pence each, it was a penny profit for me on every one sold. I set off by train to St Ives on a warm sunny Saturday in late May, but hopes fell as the two traysful of bloaters I carried from door to door became burdensome. After several hours only about twenty out of the eighty I set off with had been sold and I was tired and hungry and became dejected when people said they had "gone off" and were not fit to eat. They had become smelly and on reaching home at last that evening my sister protested at the smell being brought into the house. Father took the trays out for me to give to the hens and pigs but gave me a pat with a few kind words, blaming not me but the heat of the day. Thus my fishmongering business finished on the day it began.

Trinity Farm was so called because it was said to be owned by Trinity College, Cambridge, as was the living of St Mary's Church in Over. It was here that my lifelong friend Alphonse Mustill was brought up by his mother and his very dour grandfather.

One Saturday morning I took it into my head to walk down to Trinity Farm after the usual home-based jobs and errands were done. I was at a loose end and it did not occur to me until I was well on my way that I'd not told my parents of my intention, but Phonse was both pleased and surprised when I turned up. He was about to help to clear muck from a cowshed, and as a reward for joining in I was invited to stay to both dinner and tea. It was dark by the time I finally reached home again and for my sin of causing much concern I was to be sent straight to bed, that most disliked of punishments.

Not so on another occasion when, still under twelve years old, I was absent after dark. It was the cress selling season — January to May — during which George and I were expected to take flat wooden baskets packed with little bags of mustard and cress to sell from door to door. More of this duty fell to me than to George, not only because he was younger but because the penny in the shilling commission had less appeal for him than me. When the cress crop in the greenhouse was more than sufficient to meet the demand in Over, then it almost always fell to me to take some to the neighbouring villages of Willingham or Swavesey. Having walked the mile to Swavesey station, just beyond which the first houses began, it was another mile and a half to the end of the virtually one-street village.

On that Saturday I'd not set out until early afternoon having made a round in Over beforehand. Sales in Swavesey were not good and knuckles were becoming sore from door knocking. Swavesey people were not friendly and there must be a reason why Over taunted them with "Swavesey Scrubs live in tubs and can't get rid of fleas and bugs". I had almost reached the end of the long village and there were about ten bags out of the sixty still in my awkward-to-carry basket. And daylight was fading fast. Cussedly I went on, having always taken a pride in selling out, but having called at the last house there was no alternative to returning home with still about six bags unsold. I had nothing to be ashamed of and Father would very likely commend my efforts, and that would be compensation of value to go with the ninepence commission which sales had earned me. Besides, it was quite an adventure to have a good reason for being out after dark alone.

Soon after crossing the Briggs, marking the parish boundary at the foot of the slope up to the first Over dwellings, I heard the Crier's bell in the distance but not his voice. No matter, I'd learn what was the message on reaching home in half an hour. It was quite dark and I'd seen no one on the road since leaving Swavesey. Then close to the first house a bicycle came nearer with its oil lamp twinkling. Half a minute later the rider dismounted with, "Thank God!", for it was Father who had sent the Crier round and was now searching for me on his bike. I rode on the bike carrier home feeling quite elated, and when Mother asked if I'd not been frightened I shook my head. A picture in the illustrated Bible we had came to mind of a big bearded man with fierce eyes sitting on a rock.

"I wouldn't have been scared if I'd been Isaiah," I boasted.

It was genuinely mustard and cress that Father grew in the greenhouse. Mustard had larger leaves from yellow seeds, but cress had brownish seeds and small twin leaves of brighter green. The method was to make a smooth bed on the greenhouse floor, scatter a section with each and barely cover them with fine dry soil through a sieve. The first crop was sown soon after Christmas but took about three weeks to be long enough for cutting — less than this with warmer summer weather. Father used a sharp table knife for cutting as he knelt, cleverly grasping just enough in one hand to place in a four ounce sweet bag. These bags had already been opened up and placed in the shallow wooden trays he'd made which had hooped handles. Mustard came first to go in the bottom and then he switched over to a cress bed so that the green cress leaves topped the bag invitingly.

Being an early riser Father would have the day's produce ready by breakfast time, but before he began cutting he ate oranges. They were from the shop and were "tacked", too over-ripe to sell, but just as he liked them. So it was that one smelt not only the tang of mustard and cress on entering the greenhouse but that of over-ripe oranges and sometimes of his Country Life pipe tobacco as well. The variety of produce to be sold both in the shop and from door to door increased to include radishes, violets, narcissi and sometimes a buttonhole from the greenhouse-grown Nephetus rose of which Father was very fond, but felt he had to turn into money which so often appeared to be in short supply.

There were lessons to be learned from door knock selling. It was mostly women who responded to a knock. If refusals to buy cress came with a blunt "No," or "Too cold for cress," I did not try again for a third time. I'd begun when it was only a penny a bag but during the war period, in about 1916, it went up by fifty per cent to a penny-ha'penny. Some ladies bought two bags. A few of my best customers sometimes bought three, and these were not always the better off living in larger houses. So many houses being flush with the street made the task easier, but the few that were set back behind railings made me hesitate. Such people might resent my knocking at the front door, but to enter the side gate to their yard was risky. I did not like menacing dogs and some back yards were so muddy with hens, ducks or piglets around that I had to remember that dirty shoes were my job to clean and polish.

A few set-back houses with yews or laurels screening the window were to be avoided because the occupants were recluses or somewhat mysterious. There were, for example, two severe looking middle-aged women living in such a house to which a Major Oliver Papworth came on occasional weekends. He was a bachelor Cambridge solicitor with a King Edward type beard, an air of importance and a habit of jingling what seemed to be a pocket full of money. Sometimes he came to church, always alone, and it was said he sometimes put half a crown in the collection bag.

There were a few elderly women living alone who gave me looks as black as the clothes they always seemed to wear. Old men living alone were more friendly and one "Shrimpy" Lucas gave me some copper coins dating back to 1700 which for me were treasure. He always had a bowl of beetroot soaked in vinegar on the table, the smell from which, he explained, kept illness away. Illness was news to be spread abroad, and proof of the seriousness of the illness was sometimes to be seen by a covering of straw on the road outside the house to deaden the sound of passing iron-tyred vehicles. One had to be very considerate, but also discriminate on my door knocking rounds so as not to waste time and effort.

Saturday cress-selling resulted in knowing the names at least of everyone in the village, as well as what they did for a living. What caused people to die was also a matter of interest. According to the reported diagnosis the chances of recovery would be discussed, for in most cases the sufferer remained at home. It was not easy or possible to transfer a patient to Addenbrooke's when the only means was by cart or train, though Dr King from Willingham owned a car, unlike Dr Ellis from Swavesey.

Weeks might pass before the outcome of an illness was known one way or the other. A few made their own decisions, but they were not ill in the accepted sense. One such dropped into a well having tied a weight round his neck; another lay on the railway track for the Midlands Express to run over. And a third placed his head over a bucket before cutting his throat.

Death lurked for young people too, especially from tuberculosis or diphtheria. The former was known as consumption, of which one form was "galloping", but new treatment was then beginning to prove that a bed outdoors day and night was more likely to arrest the disease than being confined indoors. The night air was not after all a danger to health. Accidental death was not uncommon but the most horrific I heard of was a man who slipped and fell into the feeding hole of a threshing drum at work, and another who lurched backwards on to the moving cogs of a ploughing engine. Yet another was gored to death by a bull. Warnings were of course given by adults of a variety of dangers to avoid. They varied from that of damage to the hand between thumb and forefinger, which would result in lockjaw, to eating certain leaves or berries. In the Dissenters Cemetery was buried a girl who had eaten yew tree berries.

The one person in the village no one dared to annoy was Kenzie. No one "mistered" him and for all we boys knew he had no first name, for as a policeman he had the power to evoke fear which once aroused could never be dispelled. He lived in the upper part of the village but took almost daily walks to the lower Church End and High Street. If seen at a distance most boys would slink away to avoid meeting him on the path which in those days was gravelled with no kerb to separate it from the road. If avoidance was impossible, then one felt a sense of guilt which was not surprising when so often came threats from adults to tell Kenzie of some faulty behaviour on our part. At that time Kenzie was no longer young and being heavily built could have been outpaced by most boys, but one dare not run away if he shouted, "Come you here, boy!"

Kenzie said just that to me one Saturday morning in July 1916 when I was nine years old, just after I became a choirboy. It was a damp, thundery summer and haymaking had been difficult, but the crop on the big meadow closest to High Street had recently been stacked as I took the footpath to walk the mile to the river with my fishing rod over my shoulder.

With all my chores and errands done, I was feeling happy and hopeful, but these hopes were dashed when I decided to give in after an hour or two, because fish were not on the feed and black clouds were thickening. I was somewhat afraid of thunderstorms and quickened my pace even more on seeing a cloud of white smoke ahead. It proved to be the haystack I'd passed and I ran to join the little crowd already there.

It was quite exciting, for the village fire engine was there with four men working the pump on each side, up and down, whilst a chain of other people was keeping the tank supplied with buckets of water from a pond. It was fascinating, not only to see the erratic jet of water squirting on to the stack, but to reflect that the engine

30

— dated 1787 — was still functioning, though with not much effect as far as one could tell with so much smoke still billowing. I joined other boys standing by and said I'd seen no smoke when passing by on my way to the river. It was not long before Kenzie came close with a stern, "Come you here, boy!" I followed him meekly till in a space clear of onlookers he swerved and glared with, "You set that stack alight didn't you, when you went by s'morning?" I protested but he just sneered, saying I'd admitted it to other boys and an empty matchbox had been found as if to prove my guilt. He shook my shoulders, telling me it was no use lying and called to two other policemen who were coming on to the scene. It was too much and tears fell until my father came hurrying along the footpath, giving me a tremendous feeling of gratitude towards him as he brushed Kenzie aside and hugged me. He angrily told them that they should be ashamed to treat me so and that I was not in the habit of telling lies.

But there was more to come, due to an indiscretion on my part. A few days later a younger boy asked me to play with him. He lived in a row opposite the almshouses which, though cramped for space, were labelled Model Dwellings. I suggested we went along the nearby lane called Hossware (for Horses Way), having the vicarage on one side and Glebe Farm on the other. Close by the fence of the farmyard a new haystack had been built and a few wisps were lying in the lane. With these we made a tiny, separate stack for lack of other playful ideas and, just as we were wondering what else to do, Len Webster whose farm it was strode up, accusing me of being about to set light to his haystack also. My protestations again fell on deaf ears and his warnings were frightening. That evening my father said painfully that Len Webster had insisted on my being caned as an alternative to police action. His wife, incidentally, was my mother's best friend and had hinted that she would never have agreed to my being punished. Father's caning was not severe as I bent over to receive it. What touched me deeply was his apology to me for his being obliged to administer it, with just a gentle warning to be more careful of causing offence in the future.

It came as a shock to realise that I was still under suspicion when Kenzie came to haul me out from school a day or two later. I followed him meekly and full of fear but the ordeal did not last long. Kenzie sternly demanded to know precisely and truthfully all I could tell him in reply to his questions on both the burning stack and why I chose to make a heap of hay so close to Len Webster's. All this he wrote down and then let me go with a warning. To other schoolchildren I was a hero for some and a crafty liar to others, but full relief came for me when the teacher explained that the fire was now known to have been caused by spontaneous combustion due to the dampness of the hay when stacked.

That teacher was Miss Turner. She lived in a pretty thatched house on the opposite sharp bend just beyond the school. Her father lived there also as did her sister, and a daughter Hilda for whom I had a certain warmth of feeling. Occasionally I was invited for tea and enjoyed the company of all four, though I never knew which of the sisters was mother to Hilda. Old Mr Turner was conversational and knew a lot about my favourite subject, history, and in particular how people used to live, which was not to be found in any history book I had.

History fascinated me, especially wanting to know how people lived, what they did, wore and ate. I took pride in being able to repeat the dates and reigns of all the kings of England from 1066 and liked to conjure up a mental picture of people as they appeared on any given date, imagining I was amongst them. But history and several other subjects too were uninteresting at school, even when at eleven I went to high school in Cambridge by train from Swavesey station, a mile from home. At Over Church School I'd become of some greater importance as a questioner not afraid to ask the teacher whatever I chose. But in Form 2B at high school I was of no significance whatever.

I also felt a warmth towards Miss Turner, the teacher, because she was so different when at home and sometimes gave me a little hug close to her plump body, along with a smile. The only time I remember being caned at school by Miss Turner was when I had to confess to putting three dead mice on her assistant's desk, arranging them as if they might still be alive but having a rest.

But there was no smile for anyone when school began again after the summer holidays. Hilda was ill in bed and in pain, and rumour had it that her illness was due to eating unripe fruit and that she might have to go to Addenbrooke's hospital for an operation. The vicar asked for prayers, but to no avail, for within a few days the church bell tolled for Hilda's death.

Knowing that her coffin would be made in the carpenter's shop which butted on to one end of our garden, a mixture of sorrow and morbid curiosity prompted me to ask to see it. The sight and snide remarks made by the carpenter went deep and when all the school's seventy pupils went to the funeral service, I was in no mood to sing the hymn "There's a Friend for little children above the bright blue sky," or agree with "The Lord giveth and the Lord taketh away. Blessed be the name of the Lord." How could a loving Heavenly Father be so cruel, I wondered, as the little coffin was carried to the grave outside. It was all so hard to believe but one had to believe — or else. Without being specific in detail as to what would happen to those who would not believe, the vicar was very emphatic on the necessity to believe what we recited in the Creeds. There were no short cuts or easy paths to salvation or to escape the Day of Judgment.

The Way it Was

Although babies were said to be found under a gooseberry bush, only young children believed this. Not that I, and probably others, had any notion until we reached puberty at least just how babies were born, as there was a certain furtiveness on the subject. Death was common knowledge to be sure, for the regular thing was to have the church bell tolled whether the person was a church member or not. One for a man, a double toll for a woman, and a high note for children. But the arrival of babies appeared to be secretive as if by common consent. One seldom saw a woman with a pram and perhaps it was that babies were kept indoors for at least the first few weeks — or months if it was winter. This no doubt applied especially when babies were born out of wedlock. In 1916 I was much too young to know about sex and its various aspects, and had no idea why a man and a woman I once saw seemingly locked together one evening close to a high hedge in a meadow were making strange noises and movements. A fleeting thought came that the man might be committing a crime of violence, but this was dispelled by giggling laughs from the woman which left me puzzled as I slunk away, with the belief that it was best to tell no one what I'd seen.

That meadow was one of many in Bare Fen served by three "droves" named Hitherway, Middleway and Furtherway. They were all pastures in which cowslips, cuckoo flowers and even orchids grew, and where birds' nests of many kinds could be found. By the time I was old enough to understand that they were ancient enclosures from the wild fen, I also understood why that couple had secreted themselves in such a way. And, partly explained why a number of village children had the same surname as their mother. There were older unmarried women who lived alone or as sisters, who for some reason considered themselves superior. But only they pronounced their somewhat unusual surnames in the way they wished. The natives said "Cattle" for Cattell, "Mussell" for Mustill, "Bitcheno" for Bicheno, "Parper" for Papworth and "Hempin" for Hemington. Not that most of these people were proud of anything other than of a long lineage of yeoman farmers. Nicknames were of course very prevalent, and the greater the "character" they had as individuals the less their surnames needed to be used.

Emily's nickname was "Dump" and she was probably sixteen when I was twelve. So far as I know she had never been to school, possibly because she was incapable of being taught. There was always a pathetically vacant expression on her face, and her speech was little better than a mumble partly intelligible only to those who knew her. Dressed in shabby adult clothes she was to be seen walking most days up and down the street, as if she was being pushed along, with wide steps in somewhat the same jerky way as a hen. Most people gave her a cheerful "Hello, Emmy", but all they got in return was a puzzled, vacant look turning to a stare as they passed on, before she resumed her hen-like aimless walk. Only a few boys attempted to tease her — and then not unkindly, for there was so little reaction to whatever provocative statements they made and she could be no more than a bystander when a group of children played, however simple the proceedings. But I felt more sympathy for her having seen her pleasure on being given a sweet by a boy who had just before privily pissed on it.

That incident took place beside the memorial seat, just outside the vicarage garden wall. It was on a sharp bend and from the seat you could see much of Over High Street ahead and the curving road to the right with the tall church spire on one side and the church school opposite, where I was a pupil until eleven years old. Houses were huddled and some of the inhabitants were to be teased or feared according to reputation or circumstance. The low almshouses on the corner had no front doors and it was more than most boys dared to venture round the back way to one of the village pumps. For Mod Adams though small in size had a voice which matched her vigour and antipathy to boys, and she would come at us with a broom if we made a noise when taking a drink at the pump.

In the thatched double-dweller between the alms-houses and the church school lived a painter and decorator named "Pug" Sutton. Nicknames always took precedence over given first names, and not everyone knew what the latter was. Pug was not good-natured and was said to be not a good tradesman. Such unpopularity was licence enough for boys to bait him whenever they got the chance. One perfect opportunity came after a heavy fall of snow, and at break time there he was in his yard beyond a low wall, just right as a target for snowballs. The penalty for snowballing if caught was to have snow rubbed down one's neck from behind, but we felt safe from reprisals on that occasion. Pug shouted at us but we persisted, knowing he was in no position to return our pelting. Then the unexpected happened. He clambered over the wall in a rage and we scattered, some dodging behind the school one way and some the opposite way. Having reached the place where we had stood, he hesitated as if not knowing which way to go next. Then as we peeped he edged closer to the school building, half hidden, waiting. Suddenly and with a swish down came an avalanche of snow from the roof, falling on to him as the perfect victorious end of the battle. Not even the dressing down we later got from both the vicar and the teacher marred our victory. Curiously, though, it was also the end of the feud.

The Black Horse was part of another old Flemish style house. It had twin gables all in narrow red brick. Next to the pub — one of nine in the village at that time — was a ramshackle shed of wood and corrugated iron. It had large swing doors facing the road, but although they were often open, very little activity appeared to take place within. On a wet day when labourers were refused work, a few sheltered there with nothing to do, at least until the pub opened.

On windy days and often at night those swinging doors annoyed my father, for we lived opposite in Victoria House with its three-windowed shop. The landlord took very little notice of Father's complaints and when later the latter became somewhat deaf in one ear, he refused to have it syringed because by sleeping on the other ear the banging noise from the doors was much lessened. Father had been brought up to regard strong drink as a great evil and the nearness of the Black Horse gave ample evidence for him to pass on to his three sons, saying how harmful and degrading was that addiction. But I do remember him coming home from attending a sale at Somersham confessing how being both hungry and thirsty he had gone to what he called an inn to drink what he called ale to go with bread and pickles.

Victoria House was not well placed for privacy for, like many other fenland villages, most houses were flush with the public roads and pathways. Our front doorstep even projected a little on to the unkerbed path and passers-by could and sometimes did pause for a sit down on living room windowsills. The elaborate mud scraper beside the front door served its purpose and it was part of the servants' duty to tidy and black-lead it when during the winter months it was often used. Neither the roads nor footpaths were tarred at that time and the roadman had to scrape back mud into heaps or ridges to dry out before barrowing it away. Father would often exchange some to use as compost for an ounce of tobacco. The almost daily horse droppings were mostly collected by nearby residents.

It was quite an event when a road came in for major improvement. Trucks of granite stones were emptied at Swavesey station a mile or so distant, and shovelled into carts or four-wheeled road trucks hauled by a clattering little traction engine owned by Prime Godfrey of nearby Swavesey. Men spread the stones and then scattered them over with soil. But that was not all. There was no roller to press them down and it was left to hooves and wheels to compress so that, Macadam wise, each stone would end up with a flat upper surface. Lanes and paths were simply spread with gravel dug near Bare Fen for people's feet or wheels to make a firm surface. In each case mud oozed up in winter and in summer it became dust, which the very occasional motor car that came along blew up and made it unwise to have street-facing windows open. And it was a common sight to see a woman sitting on the sill of an upstairs window as she cleaned the glass, seemingly oblivious to the risk of falling backwards on to the street.

As mud changed to dust when March winds blew, so children brought out their hoops and skipping ropes, the latter being especially favoured in the school play yard. There a single rope could entertain more than one child. It was held at each end by two, whilst a third watched and timed entry while it swung rotating. But when a leg touched it to upset its rhythm, the jumper was out and the next in line stepped in.

There were two kinds of whipping top. The girls favoured the bulb shaped ones which needed only gentle whipping with string on a stick to keep them spinning. Most boys preferred the mushroom shape and a stronger whip, which if it curled sharply and firmly could set up a rapid spin, even when the top lifted itself and came down still spinning several yards away. Such tops had been known to cause injury — and to break window panes, as well as annoy grown-ups and frighten passing horses.

Marbles had little or no nuisance value. Although there was a game with them in which four could participate, it was far less popular than the twosome kind. This was progressive and well-suited for footpaths. A throw by one boy or girl a yard or two ahead left the other to see how close he could get to it. If the second thrower could span the two marbles they both became his property, but if they were too far apart the first thrower was the winner. The duration of the game as well as the distance covered depended on one's stock of marbles which, in their bright colours, cost ten a penny. It was considered bad form to cry off before one's stock of marbles was exhausted, and it was hardly ever possible to buy any back because marbles, not pennies and ha'pennies, were themselves currency.

Girls favoured hoops as much or more than the boys. They were made of rounded iron at one of the village blacksmiths for sixpence or so and, although they could be patted along with a stick, the more fortunate hoop owners had a short iron hook which gave better control, especially when at top running speed. With virtually no traffic on the village streets and roads other than occasional horses and carts, there was ample scope for children at play of which grown-ups were mostly tolerant, though cyclists were apt to chide or swear if children were a hindrance.

The girls played games which most boys disdained. "Pretty Maids", "Wallflowers", "Hopscotch" and one or two more including "Fat Bellied Doctor" as a starter for the one player to be "it" or "out".

Fat Bellied Doctor, how's your wife?
Very ill, very ill, can't you save her life?

41

> Can she eat a piece of fish?
> Can she lick a dirty dish?
> O-U-T spells out.

It struck me sometimes that girls were more light-hearted and happier at play than were boys who were much more intense, rough and competitive.

The greatest of all winter treats was when the sixty-acre pasture of Mare Fen was flooded and fit for skating. It was close to Swavesey station, a mile from home, and when racing took place hundreds of people thronged the ice. On the bank skates could be screwed on for tuppence. There were races for both amateur and professionals, the latter being those who chose to skate for prizes rather than honour, but prizes such as a stone of beef or a keg of beer had given way to money. A race course in the fen style was a straight quarter of a mile with a barrel at each end round which the two competitors in each heat had to make three turns for a mile, but the line of spectators preferred to see the race as a test of endurance as well as of speed. And when too many onlookers closed in near or beside the course, panic sometimes took over as the ice gave way under the weight. I once remember about forty people sinking up to their thighs in an ever-widening hole as they struggled towards solid ground.

Before 1916 sliding and skating for me had been on ponds within the village confines, but in that year, when I was nine, Mare Fen became a place of sheer delight two or three times a week whilst the frost lasted. But never on Sundays. Although our parents were less strict than some, having a shop imposed a duty to keep to the general rules — an important one being to avoid both work and play on Sundays. The shop also restricted my father's time for skating, but towards the end of that long spell a controversy became widespread in the village as to whether or not it was a sin to skate on Sundays. It was sparked off from the pulpit of St Mary's Church, Over, by the fairly new incumbent, the Revd Robert Lewis Ballie Oliver. In some ways he was sternly orthodox, but having come to Over from Middlesbrough was sportily inclined. To pronounce from the pulpit that he saw no harm in people skating on a Sunday, provided they did not neglect church going, was as upsetting and offensive to some parishioners as it was good news for others. Unfortunately for the latter, a thaw set in before another Sunday came. And perhaps the Sabbatarians saw this as proof of their rectitude.

To belong to a choir which was reckoned to be one of the best in the West Stow deanery, was for me almost an honour. There were two sets of choir stalls. In the chancel behind the rood screen they were for the men and boys who wore cassocks and surplices who walked in a slow, swaying procession to and from the vestry. In front of the pulpit and lectern were east-west stalls which were for women, girls and unsurpliced men, one of whom was Father when he finally embraced the Established Church.

Apart from the church, there was very little music to be heard in the village. Sometimes a hurdy-gurdy with a dressed-up monkey came to play and beg for pennies, though I have a vague memory of a four-man German band which was much more tuneful with its drums and trumpets. Once a year the Willingham Salvation Army band came with a flourish. It was always on September Feast Sunday and linked to the anniversary of the church dedication when almost everyone turned out to celebrate, the throng being augmented by people from both Swavesey and Willingham, due no doubt to relationships based on marriages between inhabitants of the three villages. It was the one day above all others, apart from Christmas, to give literal expression to the word "feast', even if most folks confined it to high tea. The old practice of eating fromenty had almost died out as more prosperity came in. Fromenty was wheat grains from the recent harvest, slowly stewed in stone jars till they almost turned into jelly.

There were of course pedlars offering a variety of wares, including gypsies who sold clothes pegs that they had made themselves. But the village was sufficient unto itself to a very large extent. Nor was it isolated with a railway station only a mile away, but Father had cause to resent the introduction of a road service to Cambridge and St Ives as did the two carriers by horse and cart. The new bus had only a dozen or so seats and was solid tyred, but it tempted people to ride cheaply if uncomfortably to shop elsewhere.

Although Feast Sunday services at church were almost as well attended as Harvest Festival in October, the centre of activity for these was near the Green on the flanking road called "Langflin" for Long Furlong. The climax of Feast Sunday was the arrival of the fair equipment.

Rumours abounded as to where it was coming from or on which road it would arrive, with youngsters on bikes itching to ride off to meet it. The distant sound and smoke from its ornamental steam traction engine put an end to these rumours, and to see it with a string of wagons behind, followed by horse-drawn vehicles and living vans, was the acme of excitement for the young. When I first witnessed this as a toddler I was frightened because the centre truck of the roundabouts with its folded down chimney looked like a cannon. Father was not one to welcome the fair people. They came to the shop for sugar, paraffin and whatnot and he no longer allowed them to settle up afterwards. Some were, he said, simply not to be trusted.

The Green was always a natural assembly place, linking as it did the three parts of the village — High Street and Church End, Fen End and the upper part known as Over End. To many the name Over was pronounced "Uvver". I can just remember the Coronation celebrations for King George V in 1911 when long tables were laid for a public tea. But I could not remember a shocking incident centred on me which took place, so I was told, when I was even younger. It was when I first began to talk — or to be able to repeat words. A nursemaid had taken me for the daily walk in a pram or "go-cart" to the Green, where some lads were loafing or playing on one of the seats. No doubt it was fun for them to hear me repeat swear words such as "bugger", but it was fun for me as well, and in spite of the girl's attempts to stop me, I continued even when back home in Mother's hearing. How she put an end to such wicked waywardness I have no idea, but

I grew up to regard swearing as a great sin. So swear words became graded in my estimation, with "bugger" topping the list, followed by "bloody" down to "damn" and "blast" at the bottom. These two crept with little shame into my vocabulary when emphasis was required in later years, until at last I paused to reflect on what they really implied. Nevertheless, it was enough to make me smirk inwardly when I found Over was included in one of Rupert Brooke's poems:

> At Over they fling oaths at one
> And worse than oaths at Trumpington.

It was when the vicar, the Revd Robert Oliver, came back from war service that his influence made some impact on the village and on me. His preaching was not inspiring, but his pastoral work was pervasive as well as persuasive. He organised a boys' football team, not confined to churchgoers since he regarded the whole parish as his sphere of duty. I was one of his team which he trained actively, still wearing his black suit and dog collar, running with us to show the tricks of passing, dribbling and shooting for goal. He acted as referee to matches he'd arranged with boys of neighbouring villages at which we were mostly victorious. Three times a week at the day school opposite the church he taught for an hour, though it was rather boring stuff about Jewish history, the Tabernacle and Temple layout, and ritual, or about St Paul's travels and experiences.

At Sunday School once a month, he would put his biblical slides through his magic lantern with darkened windows. Incidentally, my father ventured to put on a film show at the other "British" School — but only once. It disheartened him to be fined £5 for showing a chink of light, spotted by PC Kenzie. The vicar's showings by magic lantern were a change from the regular Sunday School lessons where catechisms, Collect learning by heart and what not had to be endured in the school when I, for one, longed to be outdoors.

With mention of both the vicar and Kenzie, it brings to mind the much savoured first meeting between the two. When newly inducted, the vicar made a point of getting to know his flock. Kenzie was off duty at the time and was working in what had been a much neglected garden plot which went with the house.

"Good day to you," called the vicar over the fence.

Kenzie straightened up from his digging and when the greeting was followed by, "You and the Lord have done wonders to produce such fine vegetables, from what I can see," Kenzie wiped his sweaty brow and gave a wry grin. "That's as maybe," he snorted, "but you should have seen what it was like when the Lord had it on His own."

It was not the vicar who repeated this encounter to become an ever-widening source of amusement.

Having a fairly good memory qualified me for a prize at the winter Sunday School treat. At the time I was in one of my rebellious moods and let it be known loudly that the prize book, Tom Brown's Schooldays, was not at all to my liking. But remorse set in for my bad behaviour and when, one dark evening a few days later I knocked at the vicarage door to offer my apologies, I was quite touched by Mr Oliver's forgiving response and by his willingness to change the book for one of my choice.

Concerts were also held in the church school, though not often of the musical kind. They were mostly sketches or of the pantomine type of entertainment in which Mother usually had a leading part. Father was somewhat less active on stage but was the one to provide background scenery, having the right kind of skill and a flair for painting. He could play the violin and had a good bass-baritone voice, but his greatest skill was in his oil painting of flowers, which during his middle years he had so little time to practise. My sister was the only one of the four of us who inherited that skill and it was for her an absorbing life's work.

The summer Sunday School treat was held in the vicarage garden which sloped gently down behind the churchyard to fen level. Although the house was dark and gloomy with yew trees screening it from the road, there was a large open lawn and long box-edged pathways through the rest of the garden. But Mr Oliver was no gardener and the part-time man he employed was just for vegetables and fruit as well as nuts. The latter we were sometimes allowed to pick, eating as we did so and stuffing our pockets for later consumption with fingers black from walnut stain. But the Sunday School treat proper was well organised and it was always held at strawberry time. Fruit-growing churchmen brought basketsful and there was no rationing except of the sugar which Father provided. Then followed competitions for the younger scholars and races for couples with tied legs, egg and spoon and sack races with pennies for winners until the nearby church bells chimed seven.

Much of the village was of more or less parallel roads and intersecting lanes, and lamps, though wide apart, were strategically placed so as to be seen from both directions. These were oil lamps, which were one of Over's prides, set in wind-proof glass cases on about ten-foot high iron posts. At dusk Mr Cook, who was also the cobbler, carrying a short ladder would light each lamp, knowing the correct setting of the wick to avoid too high or too low a flame. Although not more than twenty lamps were under his charge, the total distance between them was well over a mile. But lighting them was not all, for they had to be extinguished at about ten p.m. one by one, and every few days he would make another round to trim the wicks and clean the glasses.

The Cooks' home was in a thatched house behind one of the village ponds, on the outskirts of the village. Unlike most village ponds, this one was seldom low enough in dry summers to clean out. One such summer came in 1921, and I witnessed the way they took out the mud from the pond at the crossroads near the Green. The pond was used not only by driven cattle, but by horses. When riding in Father's high cart, the horse was allowed to walk into the pond to drink. The black jelly-like mud, which men with shovels threw into tumbril carts, was spread on pastures belonging to farmers who shared the work. Below about two or three feet depth of mud was a firm clay bottom. Near the far bank adjoining the Green the pond was at its deepest, and it was there that items which people had thrown in on dark nights came to light — articles which properly should have been buried in their owners' back gardens.

This village pond, which had an evil reputation, was often covered in green duckweed and the water beneath appeared to be black. Farthest from the road and nearest to the Cooks' house, there was a rushy bank and sallow bushes, under which at least one hobgoblin lurked, ready to grab at any living thing it might devour in its lair under the bank. Its preference was for children, and for this reason none of us dared to go near the pond, much less on it however thick the ice. I once asked William Cook's opinion when I was old enough to question the hobgoblin story. He looked up from the boot he was stitching with a severity I could not ignore.

"If I told you all I know about it," he said, "it would do you no good at all. All I can say is that a boy was sucked under years ago and was never seen again."

Wayward Musings

As a boy with perhaps an above average range of interests, those interests centred on the village more and more, historically, geographically and socially. I considered myself fortunate to live there and was inclined to envy those whose family traditions were deeply rooted in the village, as most of them were. Both my parents were native to Fordham, twenty miles eastward, where their parents were rival shopkeepers. The Blooms had produced five daughters and three sons; the Whitworths five sons and three daughters, one of the latter being my mother. Having been set up with the shop in Over on their marriage in 1900, the couple were regarded as strangers. Nevertheless they soon gained respect for their readiness to integrate, as much as for their honesty and general rectitude. I was the second son of a second son having an older sister Kathleen, as well as George, a younger, and Eric an older brother.

It was Eric who first gained a reputation as a likeable but rather mischievous daredevil. His outstanding exploit was to climb the ladders to the top of the 156-foot church spire when steeplejacks were in the nearby Swan, and by the time they came out a little crowd had collected down below in response to Eric's triumphant shouts as he waved down from the weather vane. The then vicar was calling for Eric to come down carefully and not to look downwards lest he fell. Only the steeplejacks voiced strong disapproval of Eric's exploit, but with George and me aiming to keep up with Eric's adventurousness, the time came when it was said that "Those Blooms'es boys will come to a bad end one of these days", and indeed we became somewhat oblivious to the risks we sometimes took.

To gain the reputation of being daredevils and prank players did not come at all amiss to we three "Bloom boys". Not that we acted as a gang because Eric was five years older than me. George and I often followed the lead he had set previously as if to maintain that reputation, and apart from a few people who resented us for some reason, there was no evidence that we were disliked by the rest.

Mrs Skinner was not amongst the latter. She never had a kind word for us and, because no one seemed to have kindly thoughts towards her, George and I decided to give her a fright one dark night. A narrow footpath called the Cramp led from High Street to the Lanes, and it flanked our little orchard behind the house. Having seen the lady — who was well below middle age — pass towards High Street, we lurked in waiting for her to come back. With white sheets over our heads we stood on the fence making noises and movements appropriate to malevolent ghosts, just as the flashlight she carried appeared round the bend in the footpath. She screamed and ran back calling down curses such as we'd never heard from a woman's lips before. We began to fear of having gone too far and of probable reprisals, knowing that her most likely course would be to complain to our parents — which she did. It took courage to go next day to offer our apologies, but having done so the surprise was that for the first time she smiled and even gave us a little jam tart.

From spring to autumn it was the river which drew us whenever we could or dared to wander over what seemed to be a very long mile to reach it. That was when George and I had to walk, but when we were about nine and ten, Father bought an old bike for a few shillings for us to share as best we could. George being shorter than me could not reach the pedals, although he could ride it without sitting on the saddle. The way we shared it was for me to sit on the carrier over the back wheel and pedal whilst George just steered from the saddle. People laughed at the sight of us but we were content and such co-ordination enabled us to reach the river much more quickly, often to venture the extra mile of "Long Drove". This was very rutty and unlevel and it led to Over Staunch which was where the river was confined to massive locks. Above and below the locks were good places for fishing, and being at the limit of tidal flow a sea based dabfish could sometimes be caught. Sea trout had also come the forty miles from the Wash and Father had been one of several who tried to hook a sturgeon which resisted capture and was finally shot.

The river had enchanted me from my earliest acquaintance with it. That was when George and I were only toddlers and when we all went together by horse and cart for a picnic. Much as Father hated shopkeeping, it was only on occasional afternoons of the Thursday early closing day that he gave us this treat. What I did not know at the time was that his love of angling had formerly prompted him to leave Mother to sleep on so as to be at the river at first light and to be back again to open the shop at nine. On the rare occasions when he took us as a family, he would punt upstream to find a grassy bank for a picnic where, at the bend known as Swavesey Gravel, there was a wide shallow for paddling. My chief delight was to peer down into the clear water from the punt to spot not only darting fish, but the various kinds of natural greenery gently waving with the current.

When George and I were old enough to walk to the river, our first attempts to catch fish were gudgeon. These little creatures would come to feed around our feet as we stood up to our knees disturbing the gravel bottom, and those we caught by dangling the bread paste bait were set free unharmed when unhooked.

A few years later, when we were able to swim, we decided to cross over because an aeroplane from RAF Wyton had landed in a field not far away. It was during the First War and such planes were often to be seen flying, but to see one land was a chance not to be missed. Wearing only scanty swim slips we found the pilot standing by who told us that he had run out of petrol but was dubious about leaving it whilst he walked to the nearest telephone, which would be Needingworth Post Office a mile away.

"Can I trust you to stay here on guard?" he asked. "I'm not supposed to leave it, but you'll do if you'll promise not to touch the controls and explain if anyone comes that I'll be back soon."

Assurances given, by the time he was out of sight we

climbed up onto the cockpit one behind the other and found the plane to be a Sopwith. An hour later the pilot arrived back in an RAF vehicle and with petrol poured in the plane took off. With the van gone we too left with prideful exultation of a tale to tell.

Inspired by this adventure we decided soon afterwards to walk to Wyton aerodrome. It took us a long time, as we were not sure of the quickest route. But from the boundary fence we feasted our eyes on planes taking off and coming down on what we learned was a training establishment — and that most recruits needed only three or four weeks before being sent to fly in battle over France. Whilst there we saw two which on landing turned upside down — a sight which was worth the scolding we were given for not returning home till nine that evening.

The little village of Holywell was barely half way by river from Over to Wyton. This too had its pub on the Hunts bank, but its ferry was little used and the drawbridge was discarded. It was not until 1920 that we came to know the place intimately. Father had not long since bought an old Krit van for business purposes but not yet learned how to drive it. But he promised to do so and to take George and me for a seaside holiday. The great day came with the van loaded with camping equipment and with Sheringham in Norfolk as the destination. Dick Bird the regular driver got the erratic engine going and off we went. But Father was also erratic as a driver, and on the slope near Mare Fen he must have pressed the wrong pedal for the engine made strange noises and then faded out to come to a halt at the bottom.

After much effort on the starting handle, the Krit

still refused to start. Begging a lift from a passing cart, Father went on to Swavesey where Ben Thorpe, who was an expert on motors, lived. Ben, a little man with a reputation as a very fast skater, drove back in a large Napier and towed us into his yard where stood a collection of ancient cars which he said were about to be scrapped as obsolete. There the Krit stayed for at least the two weeks we were supposed to have been at Sheringham. Back we went to Over to yoke Tom, our one horse, into the cart, then to transfer the contents of the van into it. From Swavesey we drove to Fendrayton to take a lane which ended at Holywell Ferry, with just enough daylight to put up the ex-army bell tent and to settle down for the night. With a hired boat and with Father to teach us the finer arts of fishing, that holiday was so blissfully enjoyable that no regrets for missing a seaside holiday entered our minds.

It was not all fishing and swimming and cooking fry-ups over a stick fire. We watched men cutting rushes, boatloads of which were hung up to dry for mat making and for coopers to use for barrel making. The rush cutting was by Tom Metcalfe who lived next to the Ferry Boat Inn. Naturally father did not enter the inn. Instead he took us to the church where, at the bottom of the graveyard, there was a brick-domed well which gave the little village its name and where one could make a silent, untold wish. On the way we passed Robert Winter's house, a painter of high repute. His full name was R. W. Fraser and he was said to be a Jacobite and therefore shunned by some people. As an artist of some merit himself, Father had respect for him and he later acquired four of his river scenes which now hang in my lounge. It was said that Robert Winter's pictures mostly went as payment for tradesmen's bills, but over the years they have become steadily more sought after and more valuable.

By the west side barrier flood bank it was less than half the distance from Holywell to Overcote Ferry because of the wide bend in the river towards Swavesey. There the inn on that side had a historical connection for it was said to have been occupied by Oliver Cromwell's secretary after his master's death in 1658.

To one side of the low mound on which the inn stood, which later took the name Pike & Eel, there was a watery thicket of silver-leaved willows. What firm ground there was was difficult to find or reach, yet it seemed to invite exploration. It must have been 1917 or 1918 when I decided to do so, having swum across the river alone, knowing that almost hidden there was a large old wooden hut set up on posts for some reason. What caught my eye was another smaller hut made of branches covered with rushes which were still green and obviously a recently built hide-out. And from this, very surprisingly, my elder brother Eric stealthily emerged. Extracting a promise not to tell anyone, he confessed that he'd absconded from Wyton aerodrome unable to take the discipline applied to cadets. He had been there for three days already, hiding much of the time, but doing odd jobs for Mr Broughton in return for food. I kept my promise but next day he came home because his fears of being hauled back to Wyton were unfounded.

There was one man in the village who took a more painful way to avoid military service. Like dozens more during the 1914-18 war, Arthur King was called up under the conscription which replaced Kitchener's demanding poster appeal of 1915 with the caption: "Your King and Country need you". The routine was a very few weeks in uniform to train, then some leave before being sent to the trenches. Arthur came home on such a leave but, having gone for a walk in Bare Fen with his gun, came back with a severe limp. The gun trigger, he explained, had caught on the wire of a fence as he crept through and had shot him in the foot. There was a hole in the boot toecap and blood stains to prove it, and when the boot was removed his big toe was badly shattered. As a man who did not generate either affection or respect, the truth of the matter was doubtless what one would expect or guess.

But for his brother Billy one was inclined to have a little sneaking affection, even though he was well clear of being on the straight and narrow. The way in which he sought to avoid honest labour and to lay hands on what was not his, was best shown in his cycle dealing and wheeling. It was finally proved how he always had good second-hand bikes for sale, which supposedly he'd bought on his trips to Cambridge. He would go there by train and come back riding one and wheeling another with a spare hand. It was always after dark, but when police suspicions were aroused by his regularity he was followed and caught red-handed taking undergrads' bikes which were so abundant in Cambridge.

* * *

Many adventures were open to us when it was not the time of year to enjoy the river. For good measure there was the pleasure of watching trains from the road bridge over the deep cutting. The line was straight and train smoke could be seen from both Swavesey and Longstanton stations. Trains had intrigued me since the time when we persuaded the maid to push both George and me in a go-cart to Swavesey station when too young to walk the mile from home. She would never wait long enough to see more than one or two, but on the cutting bank or sitting on the bridge parapet we could stay much longer to enjoy the thrill when a driver or fireman waved back, and savour the smell of smoke which wafted up to us.

To me steam was a wonderful power to behold. Engines were live things to do man's bidding just by using fire and water. Water could quench fire, but fire could boil water and turn it into steam with marvellous results.

There was another kind of steam engine which was almost too far down in the fen to visit. It was close to the river bank opposite Earith, but still in Over parish for it was the one used to drain the 3,000 acres of Over Fen when the dykes became full with rain-water. The smoke from its tall brick chimney led me only twice to walk the long muddy droves to see inside the building and to stay there as long as I dared to watch the gleaming rods turn the big flywheel without a sound. The only sound was the splash of water, for just outside was a huge cased-in paddle wheel which picked up water on each paddle from the main dyke to lift it several feet to where, in another ditch, it would add more to the already flooded river.

And this it had been doing since 1838 when Over Fen was properly drained. Over men tended the engine in shifts. Once started off it might have to keep going for two or three weeks, day and night. It worked at a slow speed but they had to keep a close watch to make sure of the right relation being maintained between fire and water in the big horizontal boiler and to keep moving parts oiled.

Albert Mustill was a threshing contractor with the equipment to serve farmers who grew grain crops. The huge box-like thresher, called a drum, was belt driven by a ten-ton iron-wheeled, steam-powered traction engine which took the complete set, drum, straw jack or elevator and chaff cutter, to farmsteads or wherever stacks of sheaves were built at harvest time. Most Over farmers had yards in the village but fields well outside the village were often scattered in the wide fen area. These were too soft for the heavy threshing tackle in winter and this was why corn stacks were made in the village.

It used to be a slur for a farmer to thresh on the field at harvest. The inference was that the farmer was short of cash and had to thresh on the field rather than make stacks to be threshed when grain prices improved. The piled-up loads of sheaves were to be seen slowly moving from a long way off, coming up from the fen. During the war, boys were taken on to lead the horse, changing over on the way up to a stackyard with an empty tumbril coming back. For one harvest I too earned that shilling a day for a week or two.

There was no pay for boys who chose to enter a farmyard where Albert Mustill's tackle was at work. It was men's work to toss sheaves to the drum feeder on top, who cut the bonds as the loosened stalks fell into a hole on the platform. It was dusty as well as noisy anywhere near the drum with its whirring pullies and flapping belts. Most noise came from the beaters in the belly of the drum which combined to make a moaning sound. On the ground at one end stood the chugging steam engine with a long belt from its flywheel driving a pulley on the drum, the shaft of which drove other pullies with belts to separate what the beaters had done to the sheaves. Grain fell out into stacks from little chutes at one end, straw was tossed out on to the elevator at the other, whilst chaff and dross fell below midway which had to be kept clear. The one whose job this was had also to take full bags away and he was sworn at if he slackened in what was the dirtiest job of all.

It took about ten men to run a set efficiently. The engine driver or the drum feeder were in charge with two men forking sheaves from the stack, two or three more building a stack of straw tipped out by the chattering elevator, one on the chaff and two weighing and taking away the sacks of grain. It was the farmer's responsibility to provide coal and water for the engine, and the usual daily charge to the farmer by the contractor was £5, though sometimes a deal would be struck at so much a sack of corn which the operation yielded.

Albert Mustill's driver, Frank Parish, was friendly towards most boys who slinked into a yard where he was in charge, both of the engine and to see that the mechanics of the drum were all functioning properly. He would allow me as a boy to sit on the tender of his engine to watch the moving parts and perhaps to throw coal in the firebox. The engine had tremendous power, and I once saw Frank pull a big old barn down by wrapping the wire rope all around it and hooking the end back to the engine and then opening the throttle gently. Slowly the rope tightened, the barn timbers cracked till all at once the whole edifice collapsed into a heap. As a small boy I stood awestruck with no inkling that in years to come I would be standing on my own engine, pulling out useless trees, roots and all.

Change and Decay

Although the heavy clay beneath most of the village made both water supplies and cultivation unreliable, it was said to yield the finest Victoria plums in all England. But if this claim was of prideful origin or of compensatory value for the fact that clay tended to make life harder, wells were still being dug to act as reservoirs.

My father had one dug in his orchard on the road to Willingham. It was about ten feet deep and, although properly brick-lined, was covered only by a wooden lid. Being just inside the gate in a patch of rough grass, it was there that Tom our one horse would be tethered to get what feed he could. But one day in the dry year of 1921 when Victoria plums were being gathered, Tom freed himself and his hind legs broke through the well cover and down he went. By the time Father found him he had settled down firmly fixed with his forelegs folded and only his head within arms reach. He was not a big horse at about fourteen hands, but though quite docile with age he presented an unusual logistic problem for Father and his helper Billy Webster.

Billy was sent off to Waymans the builders to borrow their tripod sheerlegs with its pulley. An hour later it was erected but the only part of Tom around which a pulley rope could be fastened was his neck, and this would have been the end of Tom's earthly life. The only recourse was to get the rope under his shoulders, but his forelegs were pressing tightly against the well wall. Tired already from struggling, Tom had to be pelted with little clods to make him struggle again, and at last the rope fell into position. There was no lack of help now for a little crowd had gathered both to watch and to give advice. Tom made little protest as he came up under suspension to be pulled aside and set down on all four legs. Oblivious to the little crowd he at once began nibbling again at the grass.

Horses were so much part of village life. One could tell, even when lying in bed, from the sound of hooves what kind of horse was passing. Farm horses had a slower, heavier tread than nags or ponies and one could tell if there had been rain in the night by the different sound made by horses' hooves. Ploughmen came by early in the morning, sitting sideways on one of two or three horses with supreme nonchalance. An acre a day was the stint with a single furrowed plough, and it was enough in such heavy land to return at half past three in the afternoon.

There was enough work for two blacksmiths in the village for shoeing and other jobs brought to them, and when taking Tom to be shod I sometimes marvelled at the skill and trepidity, for some horses were frisky and even bad-tempered. They could have lashed out and killed the smith at a single kick of a hind leg or bitten fatally had they a mind to do so.

The smartest horse to be seen was the white nag which brought Dr Joe Ellis to the village two or three times a week from Swavesey in his hooded cab. It was such a spick and span turnout that even the varnished wheels flashed on a sunny day. What added to the distinction was the shine of the polished black hooves against the white of the horse's coat. But Dr Ellis himself had distinction, not so much in his skill as a doctor, but in his brusquely commanding attitude to his patients. As a family we were seldom in need of his services, but having once been offered some of my mother's pastries, he made occasional calls simply to ask for more — or so it seemed. Once when Mother was out he walked in demanding to be shown the pantry, but with an air of secrecy as if he was glad no one else was there.

He came once just to inspect me when I was about ten years old. I was in trouble with irritating running sores, especially on my legs and arms.

"Must be something he's eaten a lot of lately," he said gruffly to Mother as if I were not there.

It was the autumn of that year and the final conclusion was that I must be allergic to blackberries.

"Whatever the cause," he said, "you can't go wrong if you scrub him down with soft soap night and morning."

The thought of being scrubbed was fearful, but gentle application along with avoidance of blackberry pies was effective.

Having digressed a little, there is another event which occurred during the dry summer of 1921 which stands out for some reason in my memory, despite the subject being that of the family privy. It was at the end of a low range of buildings — dairy, washhouse, coal shed — served by a path flanked by yew and laurel. The privy itself being draped with ivy was dark with no window and at night one had to take a candle or hurricane lamp.

When very young I found it somewhat creepy but was inclined to linger on the way back at night to gaze at the stars. There were other times when more boldly I would light a piece of the requisite newspaper and drop it into one of the three holes in the wooden box-like seat. Finally Father made his decision, long deferred, not only to find someone willing to take on the task, but with the knowledge of how to dispose of such a massive accumulation.

This was where I became involved, for by now it was known that I had a penchant for digging — holes especially, if only to find out what lay beneath topsoil, always hopeful of finding gravel in which there might be fossils or buried treasure. I had been growing the family vegetables for a year or two and now, with Father's encouragement, marked out a strip two and a half feet wide and twenty yards long. I zestfully dug the trench two feet deep. Then at dusk Billy Webster and another man appeared. Father set them up with cigarettes and lanterns and told us children to keep away. In any case it was bedtime and by morning the job was done, leaving behind a strong smell of carbolic around the privy and my trench partially filled in. On it the following year there grew a row of celery unparalleled for quality.

Almost every householder dug holes in their back gardens when privy buckets were full. But the four families who lived in some run-down cottages facing the builder's yard next door had to share a single outside privy. They had no gardens and not even back doors, and their bin was simply dumped into a shallow ditch at the far end of the yard which bordered on our own back garden

— a stinking, ongoing nuisance. Very few houses had drains to take used washing water or slops. These were simply emptied close by to soak away, but water was always used sparingly, whether from the rain-water butt or the village pumps, and in a dry spell the accepted maxim of "cleanliness is next to Godliness" was not easy to uphold. Those living in thatched houses had to rely on the nearest pump because they had no gutters to collect the soft rain water which was much preferred for washing days. Hence the couplet — "Rain, rain, go away, come again on washing day!"

The pump nearest to our house was often the subject of complaints. It stood at the entrance to Randalls Lane, which ended at the gate of an uneven pasture called the "Punyuds" (Pondyards) which went on to the big meadow where the haystack caught fire. Water for the pump was drawn from a well in this meadow and this was one probable reason for its erratic behaviour. Another fault was the design of its handle. This was of iron and the curve was tipped with a heavy rounded end on the principle that, with each downward stroke, its weight would assist the effort needed to entice water from the spout. But the effort required to lift the handle to the necessary height negated the supposed benefit on the downward stroke, and only adults were able to use the maximum strength required. It was also a noisy pump, but this was mainly because it mostly took several up and down strokes before any water came. The result was that residents who had no alternative source for domestic water would know when someone was strenuously jerking the handle to entice a flow of water. When the clanking ceased that would be the time to replenish one's reserves, knowing that someone else had done the initial donkey work.

"Stroddy" Mustill, however, on at least one occasion used that pump to his disadvantage. He had a milk round in the village using a little three-wheeled hand cart holding a churn with a tap from which milk was measured into customers' jugs. It was drawn from the udders of three or four cows which fed on the verges of lanes and droves around the village, for he had no pastures of his own. But when he was seen adding water to the churn from the pump, his reputation slumped further, and the result of someone telling PC Kenzie was to put an end to his business. After that most people collected milk from Johnson's Dairy to whom some cow keepers sold milk. When our house cow produced a surplus it was often my job as a boy to take a gallon or so each evening to the Fen End Dairy. The bucket had to be emptied into one that was calibrated for recording, which always stood on a flat square stone set in the floor, and the contents noted down. I began once to wonder why the bucket had to be so exactly placed since the stone was supposed to be level. Then came the chance to twist the measuring bucket round without being seen, which proved that it was off level by half an inch, to the buyer's advantage. With some glee I reported my discovery to Father who promptly took issue, which put matters right without the intervention of PC Kenzie.

This came as restoration to my self-esteem which had been somewhat shattered by a faulty experiment with milk. It was often my job also to fetch milk from

Johnson's Dairy when our house cow ran dry, using a metal quart can with a handle over the top. I believe it was my elder brother Eric who had recently told me that any liquid in a can could be swung in a circular motion without spilling. I decided to prove it but, with too much hesitation to make the complete circle at arm's length at full speed, most of the quart of milk spilled over me. I was very contrite indeed when making my inevitable confession, nor could I explain why the experiment was not first made with water in the can.

In retrospect I find it remarkable that we were trusted to seek pleasures where dangers lurked, as they certainly did along the river. The Great Ouse was the third largest river in England and Over was where it entered the fens. It also formed the country boundary with Huntingdonshire and it was here that Vermuyden the Dutchman began his big scheme for draining the fens in Charles I's reign for the Earl of Bedford, heading the company known as the Gentlemen Adventurers. His scheme included high banks to confine the river at flood time, so that by creating a flood plain of several thousand acres just above the lowest fen levels, water could be held up until more normal river levels returned. The high bank, made it was said by war prisoners, was joined to higher ground close to Over village and the flood plain included not only the nearby Mare Fen favoured for skating, but scores of summer grazing fields across to St Ives. In high flood times it was water on both sides all the way on the railway from Swavesey station to St Ives.

Close to the river at its nearest point to the village

was a large sluice called Webb's Hole. It had brick walls from which huge wooden doors were hinged so that rising water from the river could spread out over the flood plain but could be closed V-shaped against a return flow until the time came to let it go back. In addition there were a few small sluices known as "fobs" which controlled smaller areas within the general system.

Summer floods were rare but whenever one came the sight was impressive. The road from Over mounted the high barrier bank and there was a fast moving mass of water hundreds of yards wide across to the far bank. On either side were long, narrow osier beds. They stretched to the right down to the Staunch and only the tallest shoots could be seen above water. Some beds belonged to Alfred Watts, a genial bearded farmer, as well as supplier of basket-making withies which gave off a pungent smell when being peeled by pulling them singly through metal strippers by chattering women.

We boys made use of the village's natural amenities on a seasonal basis. When no winter frost allowed sliding, snowballing or skating, the temptation was to wander to where pollarded willows provided dead wood with which to make a fire. A gang of no more than five or six was enough during the year or two when I had no compunction in nicking a packet or two of Woodbines or Roll Call cigarettes from the shop, scarcely aware that I was in fact stealing. It put George's and my status favourably above that of any boy who perhaps had brought a few potatoes to roast. On one occasion we found a wounded moorhen, but it did not make good eating.

Our playmates included some Barnado boys, several

of whom were boarded with village householders. One of my own age was Percy Cann who, with another waif Tim Johnson, was boarded near the church. One Saturday morning having done chores for a nearby farmer, the pair of them entered a shed and rummaging around found a gun. In fun Tim Johnson pointed it at close range at Percy Cann's head with a finger on the trigger. The entry of the farmer with a sharp warning must have startled him enough to put pressure on the trigger and Percy fell back with part of his head blown off. Shocked beyond measure, the culprit ran off and hours passed before a search party found him, terror-stricken in a hollow willow tree trunk close to where we had not long before had a winter's day fire. He was quickly sent back to London, and a few days later the church school pupils were again marshalled across to the church for Percy Cann's funeral.

Spring was always welcome, especially for George and me with our interest in birds and flowers for which long rambles were objectives. But by June it was the river which drew us. We taught ourselves to swim — an accomplishment neither parent could impart. A bunch of bull rushes — the dark green, round stemmed Scirpus — was all we needed to practise breast stroke. They were very buoyant and once, with a friend, we decided to make a raft with them using willow branches and string to hold them together. It took a few hours to build one large enough for three, taking it in turns to push it along with a longer willow pole. We launched it out into the stream near the place where we and others bathed and swam and headed downstream towards the Staunch. Though not very manoeuvrable, it was fun with a sense of achievement. When close to the Staunch, John Gilson the publican lock-keeper warned us not to come any closer. Not only was the water very deep, too deep for our pole to touch bottom, but there would be a grave danger of being drawn to where water fell over the sluice gates with a roar and six foot drop on the lower side.

But of this we already were well aware and had dragged the raft to the bank to take a rest before pushing it back. John Gilson did not care for boys. But he was well known for his liking for beer and was trying to live down a recent predicament into which this had led him. It was a time of high flood which was above ground floor level in his house. A half-filled keg of beer had floated out of the open back door and had lodged against a willow tree some distance away. John went to recover it by boat, but strong drink and a strong flood surge made the boat dislodge the keg, and then clutching a willow branch to steady himself he released the boat to float away, leaving him dangling. But not for long because, knowing the depth of water, he let go and waded the fifty yards up to his waist back to his house and his scolding wife.

Having rested and rambled on dry land, the three of us went back to our rush raft, but we found the going upstream very different. It was difficult to keep it close to the bank because of the hindering verge of rushes, yet this was the only course where the pushing pole would touch bottom. In addition, much treading had spread the rushes and made them less buoyant. As the tallest and strongest, I did the pushing whilst George and Lenny squatted uneasily away from where holes in the raft had appeared. I turned round from my back-facing position as punter about to say we would have to abandon ship, but was shocked to note that George had disappeared from behind Lenny and there, plain enough, was the hole into the water below. To our relief, George surfaced behind the raft and we dragged him back spluttering but smiling. With each using the pole in turns as leverage, we splashed through the bordering rushes to the grassy bank, leaving the raft to drift back for John Gilson to deal with when it arrived at the locks.

We walked back to the bathing place where we'd left our clothes along the broad strip known as the Washes on which another Mustill grazed cattle, hoping there would not be a bull amongst them. The high barrier banks beyond the osier beds were also hired for grazing. Bulls were not supposed to be on the bank as it was a public footpath on the top. But once, when alone, I was so frightened to find there was one only fifty yards ahead that I ran down the bank with such speed that I cleared the wide ditch into the adjoining field. I did not quite make it because my feet slipped back on the opposite bank and I dropped in up to my waist. Scrambling up on to dry land I looked back and saw that the bull had not after all set off to chase me, which left me with a feeling of disappointment because I could not now truthfully recount it as a hair-raising adventure.

Having donned clothes at the bathing place we watched two men in the water swimming out into the midstream where it was nine or ten feet deep. Since Ridley Richardson was drowned near the far side a few years before, due it was said to an attack of cramp, few went as far as midstream, and because of rushes no one ever tried to swim right across. On the Over side there was a diving board jutting out beyond the muddy water close to the bank. Often in hot weather and especially on Saturday evenings, men came not to swim but to wash, bringing soap and towel. It was a male reserve and all who used it had to undress in full view of everyone else on the worn grass. If girls came to the river all they could do was to paddle on the gravel at nearby Overcote Ferry, mostly with dresses tucked into their knickers.

The ferry was where George and I also paddled when younger, and it was there when paddling on 4 August 1914 that some people coming over on the ferry boat shouted the news that war had been declared. Not that this meant much to me at the time, but for the next four years and three months it did so more and more with so many men being called up to fight.

The drawbridge was fascinating and built like a huge fenced-in raft, capable of carrying horses and carts or a bunch of cattle. These were being driven to and from St Ives market, for by the ferry route it was only three miles, but more than twice as far by road via Swavesey and Fendrayton. It was clever how the drawbridge was propelled. A chain stretched across the river fixed to strong posts on either side and this passed over iron rollers fixed to the side of the drawbridge fence. When loaded, one or two men took up short chains with a disc at one end and a handle at the other. With a deft throw the disc locked itself on to the drawbridge chain and pulling began with a musical clatter, so that as they leaned forward their feet became the means by which the bridge moved slowly across to the other side. When the hinged ramp touched the bottom it would rise with the slope, enough to allow the mobile cargo to disembark.

Ambitious Illusions

Compared with many other village children I considered myself to be fortunate, though this did not mean I had any cause to be snobbish. At school or at play there were no social distinctions, and even when at eleven I went to High School in Cambridge, I much preferred to think of myself as very much a country boy. But there was an advantage to be thankful for, of having always enough to eat and adequate decent clothing. And any complaints about food inevitably led to warnings that some poor children would be glad of the chance to eat whatever it was. This would mostly find its target, for not far away I'd seen Albert and Cecil Hayward eating a meal on their doorstep of a baked potato, and Albert had often asked for the core of an apple I was eating. He was six weeks' older than me and we were good friends, even if he could always beat me at marble throwing.

The existence of the shop was manifestly an advantage, especially as it was the largest by far in the village and offered a wide variety of merchandise. It was in four not very distinct sections and had three display windows. One side was for all kinds of groceries, some packeted, others to be weighed, from shag tobacco to sugar. Bacon, butter, cheese, spices, salt and vinegar occupied most of one counter but left room for a cabinet of patent medicines, or such as Epsom or Glauber salts, along with permanganate of potash which made water turn blue. Stairs from the shop led to a storeroom for the grocery side with lidded bins for flour, dried peas and haricot beans. It was much favoured by mice and therefore by George and me when we were old enough to set traps for them.

Opposite was the drapery counter where rolls of calico or curtain material could be cut to measure, as well as finished household linens, haberdashery and foot wear. Behind the main shop was an area known as the showroom where in the corner Father had to do the office work he hated. The rest of the showroom was almost entirely for women with Mother in charge. Drawers contained underclothing, but the shelves below counter level were for ladies' and children's boots and shoes on the one side, and long boxes containing women's stays and corsets which they were able to take home to try on for size. Arranged above was quite a large selection of ladies' hats. As a trained milliner these were Mother's speciality, and often with an assistant or two hours were spent in trimming plain straw headgear with a wide variety of decorative bits and pieces as well as with silk linings and ribbons.

Virtually no one was ever seen abroad without a hat at that time when more people were to be seen walking the village because, apart from Fred Kirby, no one owned a car. One other distinction the Bloom children had was that we sometimes were to be seen riding in a motor car as a treat when car owning uncles came to visit on a Sunday.

Behind the third display window was the area known as the warehouse. The window would exhibit anything from men's working boots to garden tools and tins of paint. Inside, the range was much wider from wire netting to nails, leather leggings then so popular, hoes, forks and shovels, coal scuttles and various other ironmongery as well as cartridges and gunpowder. And from here was sometimes sold home made ice-cream, made by having a block of ice sent by train from Cambridge to pack around a canister of custard inside a large wooden bucket, which was revolved by a turning handle.

Towards the end of the 1914–18 war my father bought at an auction bound copies of the Illustrated London News from 1843 to 1901. They were large heavy books and they arrived as a cart load. I spent hours poring over them and my interest in history included fashions as a result of seeing the changes there were over that sixty-year period. But now, twenty years later, fashions had changed radically, although not so much for men as for women. Men had almost given up wearing beards though and moustaches were still in fashion: Father made his come to a point on each side. He still wore stiff collars, as did most men of his status, but they were always troublesome to fix with studs, and much as they annoyed him he was reluctant to change to the incoming soft collar. But even soft collars were far from comfortable, mainly because they were so tight and made more so by the wearing of a clip pin just under the bow of the tie.

Scarcely anyone wore "low" shoes and perhaps the often muddy streets and paths were a reason why boots were universally worn, from the heavy hobnailed farm workers' kind to the more genteel button ups. For men, stiff leather leggings which overlapped the boots were considered smart if they were well polished, although to me they appeared to have no real purpose or value. Not like "gum" boots of rubber which came in later. As outer protection against rain, most farm workers wore old corn sacks, but for Sunday best navy-blue suits were for those who liked to be in the fashion and invariably a suit was incomplete without a waistcoat. At work in hot weather they might dispense with a jacket, but however hot the waistcoat stayed on as did underpants for such unlined trousers as corduroy. "Front fall" trousers were still commonly worn, as were bowler hats, both for best and at work by those whose employers had passed their old ones to them.

Only a very few Over women appeared to be fashion conscious. One of my early memories is of walking beside Mother and hearing the low thud of her ankles against her long "hobble" skirt at each step. This fashion gave way to wider, freer skirts in about 1915, but only a few years before, the florid, tight-waisted dresses of the late Victorian and Edwardian periods had held sway. The belief that hair was a woman's glory still prevailed and when, in the mid-1920s, they began wearing short skirts and bobbed hair, there was widespread condemnation from the more mature of both sexes. The prejudice against women riding bikes had died down by 1918 but at that period only a few Over women were to be seen sedately riding one. Those that cycled before short skirts became fashionable had guards on the rear wheel to prevent fringes becoming caught up in the spokes, but some also had an elastic strip from skirt to boot which eliminated the risk of wind lifting the skirt to an embarrassing extent.

Behind the warehouse were two more sheds made of wood and corrugated iron sheeting. In one in about 1915 Father installed an acetylene lighting plant so as to do away with the dim, time-consuming paraffin lamps, a dozen or more being necessary to provide sufficient light. The smelly gas was conducted by pipes to naked jets and, although brighter, there were disadvantages, as when for example the drip-watered carbide ran out during the evening or when a jet nozzle became blocked producing a thin finger of flame. Spent carbide needed to be cleaned out frequently and strict fire precautions were taken anywhere in the vicinity of the shed.

The larger of the two sheds was where Father's venture into jam making began hopefully and ended disastrously. At first, in about 1911, jam was boiled to sell in the shop and for family consumption. Fruit in both quantity and variety was easy to come by, all of it grown in the village. Batches of strawberries, raspberries, gooseberries, currants and plums were boiled in a coal-fired copper much like the one used for clothes and sheets on washdays. Then came the idea to expand so as to sell wholesale to shops elsewhere. A larger boiler was installed and boiling became more frequent. To cool off and for labelling, the jars were placed on benches, layer upon layer, with Father saying that even big factories like that of Chivers of Histon might have begun in a similar way. But in the summer of 1915 came a loud crashing sound one night, with the weight of over a ton of full jars too much for the bench to bear. Jars had smashed and jam oozed over the floor causing such havoc and loss that Father lost heart completely.

Two other sidelines however continued. One was his mail order bundles of locally-grown asparagus, specially wrapped to avoid damage. Sixty stalks to a bundle cost four pence to send, in response to advertisements in the Daily Mail. The other was the bacon from his own pigs, which he cured, smoked and sold. Not that he kept more than a few, which were brought up to the required size in a sty next to Tom's stable. The butchered carcasses were cut into sides and hams which were rubbed with salt and cured in lead-lined trays. After two weeks they were hung up in an almost air-tight hut where sawdust from the nearby carpenter's shop smouldered for another week. Other parts of the pig's anatomy came under Mother's skill to make fritters, brawns, chittlings and sausages, the casing of which were the pig's entrails. All of this went a long way to prove the saying that the only uneatable part of a pig was its squeak. Father had no relish for expanding the production and sale of bacon. Nor of the toffees he sometimes made for sale on winter evenings when the sugar supply allowed.

But after the war his efforts to prosper led him to attend sales of surplus military equipment, other than weaponry. There were auctions held in Horseferry Road and off he'd go to London early in the week by train to return with cases and bundles of army clothing, boots, and anything else he thought he might sell to the public. It was to take a selection to other villages that he bought the pre-war, French-made Krit van, but because he was unable himself to come to terms with it, he took on a discharged soldier named Dick Bird to drive it.

This investment to some extent relieved another of

Father's duties he disliked. Not that he really disliked cycling round the village mid-week to take orders from his regular customers, for he was a very friendly man and avoided persuading people to buy beyond their actual needs. But those orders had to be delivered on a Friday by horse and cart and this was the task he hated until Dick and the Krit took over. For the army surplus sales, other than from the shop, a venue in the larger villages within a ten mile radius had to be booked in advance. If no public hall was available it had to be in an empty barn, granary or even a large room at a pub.

But for all his industry, Father was not the smartest of salesmen. Rather than use sales talk and persuasion, such as a Dutch auction which began with a high price but had to come down to what buyers were willing to pay, he arrayed his wares with price tags writ large and clear. These sales took place at intervals of two or three weeks, but only for two or three years before supplies dried up. And on two or three occasions I persuaded Father to let me go with him to such villages as Somersham, Cottenham or Haddenham which were furthest away. Ten miles was for me a long way from home, and it was part of the enjoyment to be squeezed in the front seat between Father and Dick, especially when it was dark on the way back. The Krit was a night bird, they said, because its engine ran more smoothly after dark in spite of it never exceeding twenty miles an hour.

For me, Over was never a dull place in which to live, and I not only wanted to share but to play my part in what I saw as its vibrancy. One way of achieving this was to gain the reputation of being a good worker and this led me not to shirk tasks, even if they sometimes denied me the pleasure of rambling — often alone — to savour the many delights both of nature and of rural industries, being especially drawn to anything historical. This aspect became even more of interest when I learned that my paternal ancestors had been settled during the 1700s in nearby St Ives. Father's brother let me see some old books and documents belonging to one who was a freeman and merchant in the little town, who dealt in such diverse items as firkins of butter and juvenile chastisers. And there was the unproven legend that we came from Holland with the Dutchman, Cornelius Vermuyden, who drained the fens in Charles I's reign.

Although there were no distinctive rural industries in Over, there were tradesmen whose skill I could admire. Not so much that of the one-man businesses such as painters and carpenters. The two blacksmiths' shops were different for they worked with fire and red hot iron, surrounded by all manner of tools in a dimly lit, but open-doored building which titilated the senses enough to evoke a basic awe or admiration. The sound coming from a hammer upon an anvil was like a musical accompaniment, but it made me wince inside when first taking Tom to be shod as the farrier placed a red hot iron shoe on the hoof he had just scraped. Nor was the resultant smelly smoke one to be savoured.

The bakeries were not places where one could linger, but there the smell was warmly appetising and the deftness with which loaves were placed in the cavernous brick ovens to be taken out with the same long handled tools was to be admired. One or two bakers met the need of those who liked a Sunday roast but did not want to cook it themselves, thereby missing church or chapel. One saw such people carrying a cloth-covered tray to leave at the bakery, which they would take home ready-cooked an hour or more later.

There were three bespoke tailors in the village but what they did was of very little interest to me. Two of them could be seen through a window squatting on a bench with cloth over their knees, plying a needle rather than using a sewing machine. Reuben Papworth's tailoring took place at the crossroads near the Green in a wooden shed. With his chain-smoking and paraffin heater, it was no place to linger. But some young men found it a cosy place to gather in cold weather and Reuben had no objection to their company. Up to a dozen bikes were sometimes propped up outside during the lighter evenings. It seemed odd that men should do such work, and I was not very co-operative when George and I were told to visit one of the other tailors in order to make us new short-legged "knickers" out of an ex-army blanket. They lasted too long for my liking, even if they were warm with a smooth lining. It was as much against the rules for boys to wear long trousers until the age of fifteen or sixteen, as it was to have hair other than shorn. It was also the rule for girls never to have their locks cut or to be seen without wearing a pinafore. In some respects girls seemed to be more favoured than were boys, but the embedded belief that girls were less important and the certainty of boys' superiority in strength stilled most envious thoughts.

There were three or four butchers in the village, but

the Symonds brothers were the only ones with whose methods I became familiar enough to cause me some morbid fascination which soon turned to revulsion. Their premises were at the Green end of High Street and their shop opened only two or three times a week. What at first fascinated me was what took place behind closed doors on certain other days. There was no open window and the upper half of the door was left open. Looking over the closed bottom half one could see beyond the open door opposite into a yard in which a few animals stood, amid heaps of muck and offal, awaiting their turn for slaughter.

The sight of a sheep being killed on a bench was bad enough, but to see a pig hauled up on a pulley to have its throat slashed before being dropped into a large tub of steaming water was horrific. Fascination turned to revulsion at the sight, but on another occasion the open half door — which was flush with the public pathway — revealed a bullock. The Symonds brothers had driven it in from the yard beyond and, having floored it by pulling on its roped in feet, smote its forehead with a poleaxe. What happened next held my attention, for they hauled the carcase up on a pulley and proceeded to rip off the hide. But when knives began on the belly I could take no more and ran away wishing heartily I'd not been tempted to linger. Yet I had to go back a day or so later to fetch the weekly joint, for it was this same small shed not much bigger than our front room which, having been swilled out, held joints of meat and the rest — beef, pork and mutton arranged on a scrubbed wooden bench ready for customers to buy.

Apart from old Mrs Geeson who lived almost opposite the Symonds butchery, there were no other tradesmen except Mr Cook the cobbler, already mentioned, and Mr Wilderspin the harness mender. Mrs Geeson made and sold sweets such as humbugs and what we called stickjaw toffee. There were two livestock dealers. One was Shrimpy Lucas from whom, with Father's help, I bought a pig from the profit I made when at fourteen I took over the mustard and cress side of his business with his help in sowing and cutting. He and I made a sty for it and in due course seven piglets were born. At eight weeks they fetched a pound each at St Ives market, but the next batch of ten vanished soon after birth, eaten by the demented mother. It was Mr Hawkes the other dealer who bought her for £10 which I spent on a new three-speed bike.

Brakes Off

To describe Over as I saw it during my boyhood has not been difficult. Stirring the more lively of memories has led to others, almost forgotten, being revealed, including some which were less applicable to people, places and things as to attitudes, especially my own. Some of these were inexplicable and fear of ridicule or disapproval had to put them in my store of secrets because the need to integrate, to be liked, and to keep clear of the risk of sinning was all important.

It was no sin to be boisterous sometimes, nor to be adventurous, especially when some grown-ups indulgently remarked that "boys will be boys". I valued adult approbation for being of an open, friendly disposition, and for being a good worker. To myself I was somewhat proud of my early interest and knowledge of history, geography and nature, as well as of my physical strength. All such credits were, I fancied, kept under control by what was taught in church, Sunday school and by reading selected passages in the Bible. Religious fervour was so high at one period when I was about twelve years old that I even composed hymns and psalms as an outlet.

My decision to leave school when just short of sixteen was made on three counts. I'd decided on gardening as a career, and therefore it was pointless to stay on for two more years to take matric. I not only hated authority and

COME YOU HERE, BOY!

regimentation, but hated having to go daily to a town when my heart was so much in village and country life. And the tacit approval of Father who needed my help that July of 1922 was all the encouragement I needed. And the switch from short to long legged trousers, which most lads made at sixteen, was the outward proof of my inner belief that I was at least on the threshold of manhood.

From being envious of girls when I was quite young, I had now grown to disdain them with only a stifled admiration for their apparent poise and ease of speech. I'd been taught that males were the superior sex in so many ways and women were, as the Bible said, designed by God to be helpmeets to men and to produce children. At that time I had no notion how children were produced, but it was somewhere in this connection that men had to be on their guard lest they become seduced by unmarried, unprincipled women. Also in this area the term purity was applicable. Father once told Eric, George and me to follow him for a private talk. When close to the muck heap at one end of the garden, he haltingly explained how important it was to be pure, to resist impure temptations. Eric might have understood what he was referring to, but George and me at twelve or thirteen certainly did not and only years later we realised what he meant, but could not express openly or frankly.

The many changes of that summer of 1922 had the effect of dampening some of my enthusiasms. My ideas of wanting to integrate in the life of my native village vanished, as did my high falutin' ambitions for a career. Although Over had some advantage in not being entirely dependent on purely agricultural crops, fruit and flower growing was always chancy. One of the few who saw no future for himself in Over was my father. His dislike of shopkeeping was heightened by his love of flowers. Coming to a village where market growing was already established mainly for fruit, flowers were then a mere sideline. Quite different techniques for growing them were required compared with fruit, but within a few years Father acquired not only a reputation as an expert grower, but as an innovator as well. His eye for a potentially saleable kind, whether annual or perennial, gave him added status amongst other growers and this had brushed off on to me by the time I was fourteen.

I once tagged behind Father when he was showing another grower, Keet (for Chedelehoma) Hines, some new subjects he was trying out. I picked up some talk on raising new varieties by cross-pollination and this sparked off some ambition in me. It was about this time that I became far more attracted to perennials which flowered year after year than to annuals which flowered but once and then died. Father loved them all and on most summer Sunday mornings before going to church he would decorate the living room fireplace with a carefully arranged display of flowers. His flower painting had begun in his teens and, although during his middle years he was too busy to paint, his hobby came back in old age. Happily I inherited several of these paintings.

Hints came that summer that he was on the lookout for a more suitable property and to be done with the shop. His orchard and flower-growing field were over a mile apart and neither at all close to home. Nor were either of them fertile, easy working soil, and both were lacking a water supply. All this played some part in my own increasing dislike of school. I was fifteen and, although Mother was keen for me to go through the process leading to university and perhaps making the Civil Service my career, this held no appeal when by the summer of 1922 I had decided on horticulture. I wanted to be a proper nurseryman, to grow plants for sale and to enjoy the flowers.

A house and five acres at Oakington, half way to Cambridge, was purchased by my parents. Meadow House was a square-built 1860 home with six bedrooms, set back twenty yards from the road and no near neighbours. It was empty and Father and I drove there a few times in the buggy behind a newly-acquired horse and tidied up the small kitchen garden. The land was easy working and, although much of the field at the rear was planted with young fruit trees, there was ample room for plants between the rows when the time came to move the Over stocks of cut-flower perennials. But I was unsure of how to begin to be a nurseryman, and although the gardener's apron which I persuaded my dubious and probably disappointed mother to make for me was worn with some pride, it was no substitute for learning what Father could not teach me. I had to agree that I needed to go and work in a proper nursery, and thus I went to Wisbech in the August of 1922 where I was taken on by a Mr G. W. Miller of Clarkson Nursery, who grew a mixture of fruit as well as flowers and plants for sale.

During my ten-week stay I still went to church as a duty but found no welcome from anyone there or much friendliness at work. I chafed too because I was having to be subsidised. My lodgings cost twenty-five shillings a week and my wages — the going rate — were ten shillings for fifty-two hours. There was no wide variety of plants to be seen, and much less to learn about and I soon became bored with weeding and layering strawberry runners. Feeling somewhat rebellious one day, I dug a hole four feet deep in the silty soil in which to bury weeds rather than barrow them to a compost heap. Harshly censured when caught in the act by the boss, I dare not tell him of the thought I'd had of finding King John's treasure which had been lost in those parts.

Ten weeks later I was back at Oakington where my parents, sister and younger brother George were now in residence. Mother had been somewhat dubious about the move; as to whether the land would provide a living and whether she would be able to make new friends. It was nearer to Cambridge where my sister Kathleen was at art school, and for my younger brother George at the County High School. But Father was so relieved to be finished with shopkeeping and, when I joined him after my weeks of misery at Wisbech, we set to with a will on moving and replanting perennial plants from Over. It took over an hour by horse and trolley to travel the six miles. The two glasshouses at Over were also transferred and made ready for raising plants for cutting in 1923. I persuaded Father to buy ten varieties of Phlox as a sop to my personal preference, but I paid ten shillings for one each of ten Potentilla varieties just because they had a special appeal. Most of them I still possess.

Although I missed Over, I felt a strong urge to integrate

COME YOU HERE, BOY!

in village life, different though it was. Oakington as a community was much more class-conscious than Over. Only three or four families were considered to be upper class and that put us with them, because Meadow House was fairly large. It had been the base for a sizeable farm but the land, other than our five acres, had been turned into small-holdings under the County Council and split up between five small-holders. Even the farmyard with sheds and a very large barn had to be shared. This yard was quite close by, and from the first the small-holders' hens were a nuisance until we put up some wire netting. But when a cockerel flew up to settle on a post before coming down on our side, it became a target for shied stones from George and me, one of which killed it, and relations with the small-holding owner became strained. Nor were they improved when our cesspit had to be pumped out. It was just inside his meadow which ended quite close to the house, and though we had rights, he resented having the sewage spewing on to his grass and used words which indicated we were politically and socially poles apart.

Father's relief from shopkeeping prompted him to concentrate on making a garden around Meadow House once all his plants and necessities were installed. One or two of his indoctrinations prevailed, for although there was a w.c. in the bathroom, he believed it unhygienic to use such a thing indoors. He believed that rain water from the roof was meant to be used, so he had an outdoor closet installed along with a large tank to act as a rainwater reservoir.

He also decided to plant laurel bushes to replace the

gappy hedge and fence beside the road some hundred yards in length, and a selection of flowering trees and shrubs for a border beside the fence between us and the small-holders' jointly-held farmyard. For several weeks we not only dug a ten foot wide border on stony ground, but hand-sifted the soil to provide gravel for a path, Father setting a pace which for my lack of enthusiasm was hard to match. There was also the previous owner's potato crop to deal with. It had to be taken as part of the sale, having been lifted and clamped in the autumn when the market price was low. But it was no better in the spring and the whole lot of over twenty tons went for just £2 a ton.

Money was tight right from the start. Only one helper was taken on, but Frank had only one pace which was very slow indeed, and no amount of chivvying made any difference, except for the lugubrious smile on his face. As the summer of 1923 advanced I chafed and began to feel rebellious. The purchase of 100 seedling alpine plants for five shillings did little to satisfy my ambitions to become a proper nurseryman, and I chafed at having to pick flowers and fruit which Father packed for me to tie down and take to the station not far away. It was not a main line, but glimpses of steam trains stirred longings to travel. The only travelling I did was a weekly trip to a Cambridge cinema and a Saturday afternoon bike ride to fish or swim in the Ouse at Over.

It was obligatory to go to church at least once on Sundays but if I somewhat reluctantly joined the choir, I was also enticed to become an acolyte or server for the badly crippled vicar, Revd Aubyn Littledale, who needed help up and down the chancel steps at every Communion Service. But church did nothing to counteract the rebellious moods I had during that summer. The tennis court we had made after the boundary hedge and border was completed was not a success. It had needed dozens of barrowloads of soil to make it level, and it had already sunk somewhat. When George left home, I sought company with those of my own age in the village, and because most were working class my mixing with them was not approved of. It wouldn't have mattered so much if I had come in at respectable times after evening tennis or football. But when the peak of summer was over and I did not return home until after dark, once as late as ten o'clock which was my parents' bed-time, Mother could take no more of such intransigence.

"Either you change your ways," she said, "or you must change your address."

She then contacted her brother in Tunbridge Wells who fixed up a job for me at the well-known Wallace's Nursery with lodgings not far away in Benhall Mill Road, opposite the cemetery. I raised no objection, for this was at least a place where I could learn more to become a proper nurseryman. It was also, I imagined, the chance to be free and to be myself whomever I was, with the inklings that I was quite a mixed-up person with fantasies and realities chasing one another when I was not fully occupied. I wanted to be liked, but failed to realise that brashness and being opinionated were not endearing attributes, nor did my still regular church-going make me virtuous in the truly Christian sense. It was a duty and merely emphasised my loneliness as I wished I could find a damsel in distress to rescue on the footpath to and from Frant church. By my seventeenth birthday that November, loneliness, along with rigid opinions on morality, brought the first notions that real freedom could only exist in a mind uncluttered by taboos and ignorance.

It was from a Dutchman with whom I was sometimes put to work at the nursery that I had learned something about sex. But this did not shatter the brick wall of my prudery, which told me that intercourse before or outside marriage was a cardinal sin. I chafed at work, for only menial tasks came my way such as sifting and mixing composts, crocking pots for my superiors and a great deal of barrowing plants which they had prepared, along with digging and weeding. I chafed also because my wages were only fifteen shillings a week, making me still dependent on my parents' subsidy which included two shillings a week for incidentals. I was not happy and even felt out of place when spending one evening a week with my well-to-do, well-spoken uncle and aunt.

At work I was far from satisfied that I was being given adequate opportunities to learn. Washing clay pots in cold water was neither edifying nor pleasant in winter. Nor was the job of removing and replacing 120 "six by four" frames night and morning. It required two of us and my helper, Reggie, was not at all fit and strong, as was I. I finally learned that his lack of energy was due to his mother's insistence in putting Glauber salts in his tea every morning.

Early in the spring of 1924 I was not only given a half-crown rise on request, but put to work with a planter of perennials on the customary narrow beds just wide enough for two to work side by side. It was slow, meticulous work, but handling the plants themselves was more satisfying. It was also interesting to help dig out some large rhododendrons destined for the Wembley Exhibition. One other helper explained and demonstrated how he made the most use of his black plug tobacco which at eight pence an ounce was double the pre-1914 price; much of it he chewed, but only enough to make it into loose pieces which when dry he smoked in his clay pipe. The ash from this he used as snuff. Although I took satisfaction in being thrifty and frugal, I did not follow his example when about that time I took to pipe smoking and restricted my ration to half an ounce per week.

Relief came with the spring. Knowing that I was not happy at work, Uncle Harry found me a position at Charlton's Nurseries on the Eridge Road. Mr Charlton took me on to work up a stock of rock plants at double the pay I was receiving. At last I could be self-supporting and learn by handling and growing — sowing seeds and taking cuttings. New lodgings nearby and close to a railway embankment were found with Mr and Mrs Dale, he being a wheel tapper on the railway. The Charlton family were friendly, unlike the snobbish Mr Wallace who once had me ticked off by the foreman after seeing me walking to or from work with my hands held behind my back. But on more than one occasion John Charlton just laughed when I slipped up for lack of knowing all I imagined I knew.

That spring my uncle and aunt moved into a much

larger house in Ferndale Road, which had several acres of garden and woodland. In return for helping on Saturday afternoons I was allowed to make a rockery, and to join my uncle in the billiards room in the evenings. But my fenland speech prompted them to pay for elocution lessons, which I quite enjoyed even if I made no conscientious attempt to improve my speech. I enjoyed less the entertainment of uncle reading aloud after dinner on my weekly visits to Larchwood and the occasional drives in his Fiat car. Cycle rides on Sundays gave me more of a sense of freedom, for by that summer of 1924 I no longer felt obliged to go to a church regularly. What I still lacked and chafed over was female friendship, and the two or three attempts to "click", as the term was then, ended in abject failure. Why, I chided myself, was I so gauche and tongue-tied with girls of my own age, when older women were easy to talk with and some even seemed to like me.

I learned also from those who had been working at Charlton's Nurseries in differing departments, but though there was much bustling activity in some respects it was rough and ready. There was only one rather foul w.c. for the quite large staff, and it was no one's job to keep it clean. The indoor plant specialist encouraged others to urinate in a bucket, for him to use for liquid fertiliser. But in spite of it being an easy-going place of work at a wage which allowed me to save up shillings, and in spite of the hilly, well-wooded countryside, I felt an urge to move on during the spring of 1925. Adventure beckoned now that I was self supporting and I disliked town-based life with its restrictions, even if cars were no hindrance or danger to the long cycle rides I took out of working hours.

The thrill of a train journey to Yorkshire was exhilarating and to be stranded on York station most of the night on my way back from a job interview was well worth the loss of sleep. But the job itself at Malton was disappointing, for it turned out to be quite different from what my employer had promised even if it carried the wage of £2 per week. And there was a little extra as commission for manning a stall on Saturdays in York market. I also felt obliged to change lodgings after three weeks due to overcrowding and also from puzzling over the attitude of the two daughters towards me. One of them had a baby but, it seemed, no husband. I did not feel at ease and shied away enough to make relations strained, so once again I wheeled my bike away for lack of other means by which to transport my trunk of belongings.

For the next three weeks I lodged with the nursery foreman, and it was he who advised me to seek a different employer for he too was fed up with Mr Longster's vagaries. Following up his advice I found R. V. Roger of Pickering willing to take me on as propagator, and I willingly accepted his offer of thirty-six shillings a week, and lodgings which were only twenty-three shillings. Mrs Walker was a down-to-earth woman and made me feel at home even if it was primitive, with a w.c. shared with three other families. Her husband was out of work due to chest trouble and a son, living away, was tubercular and not expected to live much longer. At that time Pickering was little more than a large village, and although I joined the tennis club and later played for a local football team, my delight was rambling the moors and dales close by. In a half-hour cycle ride I seemed to be in a different world.

The nursery was run efficiently and, under Mr Roger's constant care, was rapidly expanding. His enthusiasm was contagious and with this as a spur I learned not only more about plants, but also the satisfaction of producing maximum results in the shortest possible time. A stand-up row came when I warned a senior employee not to interfere, but it was settled by Mr Roger in such a way that led to a long-standing friendship, which lasted until his death. The one depressing aspect was the workhouse which adjoined the part of the nursery where I worked. It was a grim, stone-built place and most of its inmates appeared never to be allowed out. The few men who emerged were elderly and unsmiling, wearing looks which seemed to indicate complete dejection or even fear. It was said that the Master was very strict and grasping, and had insisted on keeping men and women apart, even if they had been married for forty or fifty years before being consigned to the workhouse for lack of means to uphold their independence.

It was during the mid 1920s when I first noticed tramps trudging along main roads, and at Pickering learned how many walked from one workhouse to another, preferring or not being allowed to reside in any one of them. Their numbers increased after the 1926 General Strike, followed by the Depression; so did the number of intinerant pedlars — most of whom had hard luck stories to tell. Some were told with bitterness —

how, after surviving the war and its horrors of trench life, they had been thrown out from normal life by a thankless government. I'd grown up to regard tramps as the dregs of humanity through their own laziness or addiction to drink. I'd also seen men picking up fag ends from Cambridge gutters, a practice observable up to World War II. So it was that I felt less pity for those approaching Pickering along the lonely Whitby road than for the few regular inmates of the nearby workhouse out for their brief spell of freedom. The name workhouse seemed to me inapt for, although I did not know of any work they had to perform inside, there was also no garden in which they could have found relief and perhaps more besides.

There was a marked difference to be noted between the natives of the three localities with which I had become familiar — of fenside Over, Oakington and North Yorkshire. There was a kind of vigour in Over where, in spite of difference in social or financial standing, there was a noticeable lack of respect between master and man. At heart Jack reckoned he was as good as his master and scarcely any worker addressed his employer with a "sir". At Oakington the latter was more or less the rule, and junior members of an employer's family were addressed with the "master" or "miss" prefix. At Pickering there were scarcely any distinctions of that nature, for it appeared to be uncalled for where the norm was to say what was needed with a bluff directness. That Yorkshire people called a spade a spade contrasted sharply and sometimes disconcertingly with my more calculated or devious fenland approach. This

100

sometimes brought out a puzzled look on the face of a Pickering person when I was phrasing some request or whatever. It often led to the person breaking in with, "What you mean is . . ." or "Are you trying to tell me . . ." I was an East Anglian but much as I longed to see more of the world, I longed even more to become a nurseryman, to rejoin Father, and I worked hard to attain that end. For a village boy to break away as I had done was against custom and tradition.

Helter Skelter

My parents had obviously become fully integrated in village life at Oakington when I rejoined them in January 1926. Father had become a churchwarden and Mother a leading light in the newly formed Women's Institute. And she had formed a close friendship with the newly widowed Mrs Philip Papworth of Westwick Hall. My brother George had finished schooling and had been persuaded to go to London to live with the joint owners of a printing works belonging to old friends of my mother, who were childless. Kathleen was at Homerton College in Cambridge, reluctantly training to be a teacher for lack of openings in art. Whilst I felt quite mature at nineteen, it was partly because of my absence from home of three years. Now I was of the master class and this carried certain obligations, especially with those working for us who were told to refer to me as "Master Alan".

Frank Stearn had been the first employee and was still there. He was a few years older than me, a willing affable type, but slow in speech and movement, so slow that we sometimes teased him. He was so ungainly that he could neither run nor ride a bike. It was almost a joke that he was allowed to stay, especially as Father was so swift of movement. But, apart from his liking for village gossip, Frank had a kind of naive innocence which held one back from being harsh with him.

Although work came first with me, I also wanted to

join in the life of the village. The taste of freedom from obligatory churchgoing had some effect on me and I had no inclination to rejoin the choir. Sunday work though had to be surreptitious, and even my parents believed it should remain a day of rest with at least one church attendance. There was criticism of the upper class Webbs at Oakington House who were actually seen tending their garden and playing croquet. Those who attended the one chapel — the Strict and Particular Baptist — were known to uphold that title so far as Sunday Observance was concerned.

Apart from the washerwoman who came on Mondays, Mother had managed so far to run the house alone. Mrs Chapman was also one of two women who were employed for flower picking in season, but in 1926 it was decided to have a young girl as housemaid. Nellie Swain was about sixteen and her weekly wage in addition to keep was half a crown to begin with, out of which she had to pay for part of her cap and apron. But Nellie soon proved to be a bad choice by Mother's standards. She was too familiar and, although I'd not been aware of it, she was suspected of being a corrupting influence on me. After a month she was sent packing to be replaced by more daily help from the other flower picker, Mrs Smith, at sixpence an hour, the going rate for women compared with Frank Stearn's thirty shillings for his fifty hour week.

Changes were afoot in 1926, so were modern inventions affecting village life. The wireless was one of these and it was thought quite magical how, by prodding a crystal in a little box, one could hear voices and music through the headphones. And two pairs enabled the wireless to be shared, all powered by electricity in a glass battery and caught somehow as the invisible sound rays touched the wire aerial between two chimneys. News came that spring, both by wireless and the *Daily Mail*, that a national strike appeared to be inevitable. And so it proved, to be much resisted and regretted, for our crops depended on railway transport to distant markets. I volunteered to act as guard or fireman, but the Cambridge railway authorities told me that so many undergraduates had been taken on there was no need for more. I felt quite disappointed.

The later 1920s were hard times for almost everyone who strived to make a living from the land. We were no exception. My ambition to grow and sell plants in quantity and variety had to be curbed for lack of capital. But Father agreed to buy a van to enable me to put up exhibits at flower shows to attract orders and to have a stall on local market days. It was a solid-tyred Trojan, powered by a two-stroke engine chain drive with a top speed of 30 m.p.h. It was the beginning of the end for our use of horse transport, though Father still preferred horse and buggy even if it was becoming more difficult to find stabling when used for trips to Cambridge.

There was most evidence of poverty in families where there were several children. Those from Westwick had to pass our house on their way to school and the clothes they wore were indicators. Hand-me-downs were much in evidence, and yet on Sundays they were much more carefully attired. But Frank Savage reserved his best clothes for Cambridge market. He lived in a very old thatched house set in an untidy, muddy yard, in which a few hens and geese roamed. Both he and his wife were above middle age, he with a wispy beard and she with hair tightly drawn over her scalp. Frank's gaunt appearance went with the impression he tried to give of having seen much better days as a merchant rather than the dealer he had become, for now he had just a sprinkling of other people's surplus fowls, eggs and vegetables to supplement what little he had of his own to sell in Cambridge on commission. And for this he dressed meticulously with starched shirt front and a black cut-away morning coat.

It was in the summer of 1926 that a sprightly middle-aged man called to offer Father his services in such a way as to persuade us that we needed him. And so we did, for "Sailor" Smith very soon proved his worth. He preferred garden work to his present job at Manor Farm where he drove one of the two tractors in Oakington. Sailor was much like Father in age and ability, but with a sharp tongue which soon found a target in the slow motion of Frank Stearn's pace at work. Everything Sailor did was full of zest, with an ever open mind for the most effective way of tackling a job, and from him I learned such skills as mowing with a scythe, laying bricks and drainage pipes. Sailor Smith was unusual in his ability to talk whilst keeping up a smart pace at work. I enjoyed listening to his tales of navy life — which was the origin of his nickname. He had spent sixteen years at sea from the age of fifteen in 1886 until 1902, with service in the West Indies and the Far East. A native of Oakington, his parentage and boyhood there was a closed book, but he was a keen judge of human nature and, although he was a fairly regular attender at the Strict and Particular Baptist Chapel, he spoke of it almost jokingly. He was especially critical of the then pastor, a Mr Rowell, who kept a clothier's shop in St Ives and who, as a "Bible puncher" laid much stress on what would befall the sinners in this life when they were transferred to the hereafter. Sailor's only expletives came out when he was annoyed or frustrated — "Hells bells and panthers tracks!", "What the bladder of lard?" or "Goodnight and little apples".

Also unusual, but in a very different way, were the Mitchell brothers. Between the four of them they ran a smithy, wheelrights, undertakers and wagon builders' business at the crossroads in an old, rambling set of buildings. All were above middle age yet the two youngest were masters over their elders and, when I took our horse to be shod, I could feel sorry for kindly old Ezra there in the dim light pumping the bellows for his younger and sturdier brother at the anvil. Next door there was Edmund, the youngest of the four, lording it over his brother Reuben in the carpentering section. Or so it seemed, and Sailor also confirmed this impression.

The older Mitchells would smile but seldom spoke, but Edmund on occasion would open up in a slow, somewhat complaining way of speech, especially if I showed some interest in the vast array of ancient equipment and piles of sawn timber. "Them's fellies for cart wheels and them's for spokes," and "There's a pile of hubs over there, but farmers don't want new carts much nowadays." These stock piles, he explained, had been cut up to twenty years ago in expectation of need and to ensure stability. "We used to buy a tree according to what the wood was for, 'cos it had to be different wood for different purposes," he would say. I asked him about the piles of broad planks with air spaces between each, but with the original shape of the tree trunk in sections. "Them's coffin boards, mostly ellum, but they were cut by hand in a pit — one man in the pit pullin' downwards and tother on top pullin' uppards. Have you got a use for any? 'cos I doubt if we'll ever use 'em all up. I even bought one of them band saws to make it easier work, but we never use it now."

When I said I could see no horticultural use for coffin boards he grinned. "Din't think they would — but what about a brand new wagon? Be a lot better for you than that tew wheeled trolly of yourn. Come along o'me and I'll show you. Brand new it is."

Edmund opened a shed door and there it was in somewhat faded blue and pink paint. He then explained that it was made in 1897 for a customer who died that same year. He also explained that it was a "hermadite" wagon, which meant that it could be taken apart to use as a two-wheeler for muck or sacks of corn, but as it stood it was a harvest wagon with raves to enable wide loads of sheaves or hay to be piled up.

"Ah well," Edmund said with a wan smile when I declined his offer, "I never thought you would, but if you hear of a likely customer — it's brand new."

Edmund did not live at the nearby house, but down the road where his wife was the village postmistress. She was a prim and proper lady on whose face I never saw the vestige of a smile. They had no children and it was said they had been engaged for eleven years before marrying. With them lived her brother, Harry Willson, who gained an indifferent living as a painter and decorator. It was also his job to deliver telegrams, for at that time scarcely anyone had the telephone laid on. During the flower cutting season it was Harry who often came with the little brown envelope. "Tallygram!" he would call out, and would sometimes add as he handed it over, "Don't know wass in it, but she says it's about what your flowers fetched at Birmingham (or wherever)" — "she" being his sister.

It was during the 1920s that Jonah Dellar took over the bakery from "Beggar" Papworth for whom he had worked. In his quiet way Jonah was more ambitious and branched out into baking a wider variety, including the new "Vitbe" malt bread and what he called "fancies" (little cakes with pink or white icing) and rather tough doughnuts. Ordinary bread was somewhat disdained even if it was still in demand, judging by the way it was handled. It would be tossed from the bakery door and caught by the man who tossed it into the delivery cart. Sometimes a catch was missed, but picked up from the road it still went in with the rest. And on one occasion I saw his young son kick a loaf around the cart before being told to pick it up by hand.

Another man for whom I and others had an affection was George Doggett who lived in a brick house opposite the school. It had been built, he told me, for exactly one hundred pounds in the 1870s by his father. George was elderly with a white beard and a limp, which did not prevent him from walking most days past Meadow House to the adjoining farmyard where his son Bert farmed as a smallholder under the new Council scheme. Bert had chest troubles and very little energy — or, for that matter apparently little else in his favour. But the very good looking Olive Clayton, who had both energy and personality, decided to marry him. And when Bert died after a few years she took over and became a very successful farmer.

At the time of writing Olive Doggett is still alive, but in retirement, living in a house which in the 1920s was occupied by an elderly lady with a forceful character named Martha Harradine. She had long been widowed and once, looking through the church register, I saw the record of her marriage in 1866. My paternal grandmother sometimes came to stay at Meadow House and Mother invited Martha to tea, thinking they might find it of mutual enjoyment. They did until Martha invited Grandma Bloom back to her house. She never went, for Martha had promised to make one of her "tipsy cakes" as a special treat, which went much against Grandma Bloom's principles as a strict abstainer from alcoholic liquor.

The end of the 1920s marked the end of my parents' residence in Oakington. For various reasons, not least to allow me to take over the holding when I wished to marry, they moved to Mildenhall late in 1930 where, after restoring a dilapidated glasshouse nursery, Father devoted his time and skill to indoor plants. My brother George had not long since become fed up with a career as a printer in London and he too joined in the new

Mildenhall venture. By 1934 all market flower growing at Oakington had gone in favour of wholesale production of perennials and alpines.

My reasons for switching over to wholesale production were chiefly personal. I found I disliked retail selling both at market stalls and at flower shows. Even exhibiting at the Chelsea Show in 1931–33 made me chafe and admit that I not only preferred growing to selling, but also that I was a very poor salesman on the one-to-one basis. This sparked off the belief that if I grew the best possible quality plants in good variety at reasonable prices with efficient service, orders would come from retailers with whom I was not in competition. And so it proved, for by 1936 all my fifteen acres were full and I was looking for more land.

This was a period of almost total enthusiasm. I dug two wells for irrigation, laid drains where needed, raised some new varieties as well as widening the range by other means. My 1939 annual catalogue listed 1,870 items with thirty-six helpers for the then thirty-six acres of plants. This included an old nine-acre orchard a mile away which I acquired by having to dispose of the trees in return for a rent-free year.

Then I got the idea of competing with the Dutch who were exporting large quantities of hardy plants to Britain. I hired some land similar to theirs in Lode Fen a few miles north of Cambridge. As a trial it was a failure, for having planted four acres a flood came soon after, which stayed long enough to drown the lot. Cussedly — and in spite of gathering war clouds — I looked around for similar black, easy-working soil to purchase rather than hire. I'd had a profitable venture with the then new Korean chrysanthemums and when offered a 200-acre farm in Burwell Fen for £1,600 I found the challenge irresistible.

The Hidden Forest

It might be helpful at this stage to describe the topographical background to the fens on which this record of a past age is based. The fens at Over were alluvial as a result of being close to the River Ouse which, with frequent flooding over many centuries, allowed muddy water to build up the surrounding soil level well above the basic clay or gravel. It was a heavy substance and lacked what farmers called a "staple" — or defined subsoil. Much further north the alluvial soil was of a very different type because there it was sea floods coming inland which, as they receded, left a silty deposit easier to work because of its sandy content. As a boy it was the intervening type — the Black Fens — that intrigued me, because the soft peat had been built up from decaying growth of reeds, rushes and sedge to a depth of up to twenty feet in places. And some had been a forest of oaks which had flourished before water levels rose (or land levels sank) over 4,000 years ago, which appealed to my boyhood imagination. Drainage, farming and turf digging for fuel made much easier by steam power had brought the preserved oaks nearer to the surface. Little did I imagine, however, that it would be my lot to deal with one of the last and largest traces of that ancient forest and to be the destroyer of a 350-acre patch of wild fen adjoining the 200-acre farm I bought, most of which had never been cultivated.

I found that the Burwell Fen Drainage Board was not only inefficient but that it was close to bankruptcy; yet it was not waterlogging which made the few acres of nursery plants useless. They grew well during the summer of 1939, but with the onset of war orders dried up. And then followed the wartime rule that decorative nursery stock must be reduced to one sixth in favour of food crops.

This plunged me up to the neck in farming, the skills of which I had much to learn, and the switchover brought my finances to rock bottom. The farmstead was over half a mile down a fen drove — dusty in summer and so muddy in winter that I had to leave my car where the hard road ended and walk. Water-filled ruts were so deep that cart wheels would sink as the soupy black mud engulfed them up to the hubs, and in such unstable soil it was not safe to drive near the narrow grass verge because of the bordering ditches on either side. It was a bleak landscape, treeless but for a few pollarded willows and cheerless when the winds blew, as they mostly did without hindrance.

The farm was sold to me by a Mr Greenall on behalf of his widowed daughter. I'd believed what he'd told me about it, but later found that if he had been decidedly economic with the truth, he had told me no downright lies. I did not haggle over the price. Eight pounds per acre was cheap even if an extra pound in annual drainage rates had to be considered, and it compared favourably with good upland farm land at the then price, including a farmstead, of forty to fifty pounds per acre. Not that this farmstead was comparable because the buildings were of wood and corrugated iron, and the house was more of a cottage and very isolated indeed, with evidence that the land was shrunken due to wastage of the peat on which it was built.

Its occupant was Sid King, the farm foreman, with a wife and young daughter for company. Sid agreed to stay on although he had been there less than two years, at his current wage of fifty shillings a week. This seemed high to me when the regular farm workers' wage was thirty-six shillings. But I soon found out that Sid was no ordinary worker, willing to do only the regulation fifty hours a week. He also appeared relieved to have a new boss, even more so when I told him I was new to farming and had much to learn. He quizzed me about the deal and then with a grin reckoned I'd not done too badly, because it was said of Mr Greenall that when the time came the undertaker would have a job to get him into a coffin on account of him being so crooked.

Sid had forsaken farming his smallholding a few years before when times were bad in favour of contract work with a horse and cart for the county council in improving roads. His job was to cart granite roadstone from the nearest railway yard up to five miles radius. First the rail wagon had to be opened and out poured a heap of granite on the ground. From there it had to be thrown up with a special fork on the cart, and then Sid and the horse with a full load walked to the site.

It was soon obvious to me that Sid had something of a chip on his shoulder. I guessed it might be due to his having lost the status of being his own master, even in a small way, to take on such an isolated farm under the critical, know-all Mr Greenall. But, because at thirty-two I was not only much younger than him and rather a novice to farming, he rather welcomed the opportunity of making me dependent on him. So it was that in matters of which crops to grow where and what were the priorities, it made sense to defer to him. This included the purchase of implements needed and taking on more help, although two regular men had stayed on with him. One of them was George Johnson, who was an expert ploughman with horses, and Sid agreed that he should plough up some rough grazing land which lay between the drove and the embanked river known as Burwell Lode and which had not been under plough for at least forty years.

I'd made a point of being there soon after the work began, partly out of curiosity. The sight of what lay under the surface had always fascinated me and this was a new and exciting experience. The plough was a single furrow, deep digger type, and apart from the skeeth — an attachment which cut through the turf ahead — a skim coulter was in position as well. This was a flat, hand-shaped scoop which lifted the turf at about three inches deep so that it dropped into the open furrow bottom to become buried upside down with the bulk of soil turned by the deep plough breast. George had just set the opening furrows as a ridge, one furrow against the other, at a fairly shallow depth and now would adjust the plough to dig in at the full depth of twelve to fourteen inches. I walked behind, watching the black earth being heaved up and over, oblivious to the plaintive calls from a plover and the drumming noise of a disturbed snipe. The furrows were about 200 yards in length and the field dead level except for a short rise close to the river bank. There George with a tug on the cord fixed to the bridle of the outer of the paired horses called, "Watch!" Smart knew what it meant and began to turn with Blossom having no choice but to turn with him. By pressing down on the plough handles it rose up out of the furrow and once out George, with minimum of effort and control of the horses by the cord, turned the plough to begin the reverse process. But half way back there was a low thud and both horses and plough came to a dead stop. George turned back to me with a grin. "You said you hoped we'd find a bog oak — though I didn't think why. Well, that's what we've hit and it may not be the last. Spoil my work they will with having to be pulled out by tractor."

A spade was lodged on the plough and now I could see why George had brought it. He prodded down and then traced the trunk for its length and direction. "Not tew big," George muttered. "But I'd better put a stick or two in to mark it and a wooden dowel in the hoss trace in case there's more, so it snaps the dowel rather than bust a ploughshare. If there's one there'll be more, and I'd lay a shillin' on that."

George was clearly disappointed knowing that the more bog oaks there were, the more they would spoil the appearance of the work in which he took such pride — all the more so because he obviously wanted to impress me. This trunk was only about five yards long and about two feet in diameter, but it was hard and heavy. By the end of the day's work he had hit two more and having taken on two more helpers, they laboured for a week after the ploughing was finished by digging round each one and cutting sections with a cross-cut saw. It was then possible to roll them out on to the surface to be dragged away with a tractor. It took most of two weeks to clear the oaks from that field, to level it, harrow and firm it by rolling, before oats could be drilled as the first crop.

I'd thought of bog oaks as one of the exciting features of the Black Fens. They had lain there for at least 4,000 years, after slowly dying from some great flood and gradually being covered as peat built up from decaying marsh and aquatic vegetation. But little did I imagine in 1939 what lay ahead and how my views would change. Less than two years later I had let myself in for clearing and farming an additional 350 acres adjoining my own 200 in order to produce food crops. Much of it had never been cultivated, having been abandoned after levels had been lowered by turf cutting for fuel. Scarcely any more had been dug after 1914 and the serried cutting trenches (known as pits) were water-filled in winter, overgrown with reeds, sedge and sallow and other bushes. It was, in fact, a wilderness and the National Trust had taken it over to add to its well-known Wicken Fen Preserve close by.

It took three years to bring that part of Adventurers' Fen under crops but about two acres had to be set aside as a dump for the hundreds of bog oaks we found. Some were huge with trunks up to eighty feet long and five feet in diameter. We also found boar tusks and deer antlers, but once exposed the oaks began to deteriorate with fissures appearing. The wood was so hard that no one wanted the task of sawing it, and it made poor firewood. News did, however, reach a Midlands man who took two lorry loads for making antique furniture. I was glad enough to give it away, but as a token he sent me two jars he made from it which I still possess.

This reclamation — said to be one of the toughest ever undertaken — was under the auspices of the War Agricultural Committee. They gave me a free hand and I was able to charge costs to them, but the extra machinery and equipment and additional labour required were my responsibility. Most of the latter came from Wicken and Soham rather than from Burwell village, but Stewart Collins lived in a shack on the edge of the fen close to Wicken Lode, which, with Burwell Lode, formed a large V enclosing the whole area now under my control. Stewart was however, not the kind of man who liked to work with others but preferred to take on piecework on his own. One reason for this was that after a bout of beer drinking he would be laid low for a few hours, or a day or two. On one occasion he was off work for three weeks, having fallen off his bike on his way home at night. For crushed ribs he took large doses of aspirin, refusing to seek medical help. Stewart Collins' gruff attitude was bordering on fierceness as if, for him, attack was the way to assert his independence. I first employed him to dig a new ditch, but even after agreeing to his piecework price per chain length (twenty-two yards), he gave the impression that any criticism would be resented and that in any case I was getting the job done on the cheap. It was, therefore, almost impossible to talk with him as man to man and, much as I wanted to know more of what he could have told me about local history and the old turf diggers, his only concern seemed to be the job in hand from a purely personal angle — his skill and the reward for his use of it.

The other workers regarded him as odd, but one to placate rather than annoy with criticism or disdain, although dark hints of his home life were a matter of secret amusement. His single story shack had only two rooms and conjectures were made on how Stewart's wife, two sons and two daughters could all live in such close, primitive proximity. Those offspring, as well as his wife, worked on the land here and there, now and then, some of them for me on the sugar beet — and quite good, cheerful workers they were, but the sons especially gave the impression of being completely dominated by their father.

The Farm in the Fen

My first year as a fen farmer revealed that I had not only much to learn about farming, but also about those who did the seasonal work on the land. I wanted to work with them to learn their special skills, but when I tried to do so I met with more tolerance than approval. It was the practice when a corn crop was ready for harvesting to mow a swathe with a scythe around the field, to make a space for the self binder to come in for the rest. It not only needed a very sharp scythe, correctly wielded, but the tying by hand of a bunch of stalks into a sheaf by twisting a few stalks to hold it together. But the knack of doing this, so easily performed by others, eluded me. There was no part I could play until the binder came in. It was a machine which cut about a four-foot wide swathe with rotating "sails", which swept the loose stalks into the body of the machine to emerge as complete sheaves tied with string ready for stooking. This I could help with, gathering two sheaves at a time and placing them against one another till with about ten, a stook was complete with corn ears uppermost to dry out until ready for carting off and stacking.

My next lesson to be learned was when I decided to help loading sheaves on to carts as they went from stook to stook. With more energy than forethought, I tossed sheaves up for George Barton to arrange in formation so as to carry the maximum load. But my pace was much too fast for him to handle and, with a pile around his legs, he glowered at me with, "Either you take my place up here — or you slow down. Which is it to be?" With an apology from me work began again, with the seemingly slow rhythm which years of experience led to a job being well done. Sid King was also a fast worker and at times a cussed streak in him emerged. One evening two loads of oat sheaves were left in the stackyard when the others had knocked off. The unloading could wait they said till morning, but it worried Sid to see them there with no tilt to cover them if it rained. Rather than spread tilts over, Sid decided to unload them if I was willing to help him. I'd had enough and wanted to get home, but felt I had to give in. Some stalks were still green enough to cause me misgivings, but Sid was insistent. Ten days' later that stack had to be remade. It had begun to heat and even if it had not caught fire through spontaneous combustion, the yield would have been spoiled. "Carted too soon — that were the trouble," Sid complained, as if it were my or someone else's fault.

It was from the two oldest of my helpers that I learned more about the turf diggers who, over thirty years before, had been the only workers in Adventurers' Fen. This name, incidentally, arose from the "Gentlemen Adventurers" who put up the money to drain the Black Fens in the reign of Charles I. They were headed by the then Earl of Bedford and as reward were able to share amongst themselves some 90,000 acres of what became known as the Bedford Level. But until steam power came 150 years later, quite large areas were not well enough drained by the only power available, although even partial drainage allowed the peaty soil to shrink. Windmills abounded — as one would expect from a Dutch overseer for the scheme — and it was said that there were so many in Burwell Fen that there was not enough wind to make them all work at the same time. Only one remained now, standing idle on the area being described.

Billy Norman and Shady (for Shadrack) Simkins told me how turf diggers in small gangs made themselves huts of sods with reeds for the roof, in which to live for the working week. Landowners stipulated how deep they were to dig, measured by the standard fourteen-inch turf. Having pared off the surface growth, they made trenches with spaces called "staddles" between, on which to stack the turves for drying, and when dry in late summer or autumn they had to be barrowed away — mostly to the nearest "lode" for transport by barge. Merchants then arranged to sell them in towns and villages, but at nearly double the price the landowner had paid per thousand turves to the diggers on piecework. Billy and Shady spoke of how rough and primitive the conditions were under which the diggers lived and how, before their time, it was known that one digger murdered another. But neither the murderer nor the body of his victim was ever brought to light or justice. It was easy enough to guess that somewhere in this wilderness the skeleton of the victim might be revealed when the deep digger plough came in, or when one of the many new ditches required were dug, and it was obvious that Billy and Shady shared this thought.

Turf digging inevitably led to land being abandoned.

If it was rendered too low to be drained, the owner was then relieved of the obligation to pay drainage rates, and this of course put an extra burden on the Drainage Authority and on those who continued to farm. This is precisely what had happened to Burwell Fen. There was, however, one crop which could be taken from unfarmed land other than turf. It was the natural growth known as "fen litter", which when mown and cut into chaff went to feed the thousands of London horses which were the mainstay of transport prior to the early 1920s.

Tractors obviated the need for more than two horses on my farm, but they were useful for both hoeing young sugar beet and carting it when harvested. Much of it went by barge to Ely Beet Factory, but a sad loss occurred due to the carelessness of the man leading a tumbril load of it when crossing a wooden bridge over a wide ditch. He allowed the horse to walk too close to the edge and one cart wheel went over. The weight of its load pulled both cart and horse over and they fell in. The horse was pinned down by the shafts and drowned, but the loss was compounded by the fact that the horse was on trial from a local dealer and I had to pay the forty pounds he'd asked.

Ditching men, apart from Stewart Collins the loner, preferred to work as a gang of four at piecework by the chain length of twenty-two yards, which was usually a good day's work. Field ditches were usually eight to ten feet across, sloping down to half that width at the bottom. The depth varied according to the lie or level of the land, which depended on the direction in which the water had to run to link up with the overall system before being pumped up to the embanked river — often a lift of ten or twelve feet. First, the growth of reeds, sedge and other plants such as willow herb and meadowsweet had to be pared off. Below, the digging was easy until water came seeping in. To overcome this, a "stank" or dam had to be made at the end of each section to keep water out and to bale out any excess in the section itself. A newly dug ditch with smooth, even sides was always in my estimation a tribute to the men who made it. None of the machines which came later could do such perfect work. However, a hydraulic digging tractor or a dragline excavator could do with one operator three or four times the length in a day of what four men could do.

The roughest and hardest part to be cleared was known as "Rothschild's Thirty Acres". It was in a square block and if ever it had been dug for turf, it would have been long ago, for it was so thick with bushes — sallow, quickthorn and buckthorn — as to make it almost impenetrable on foot. This was why it was the last area to be tackled and extra men had to be taken on to cut and burn the bushes before tractors could pull out their roots. Burning was cautiously undertaken because a fire on peat soil will burn insidiously downwards. Almost all the thirty men employed hacking away knew this and, once a fire had died down overnight, the ashes had to be scattered and the site dug over next morning. Once it gained a hold, a fire "pitted in" could burn down to water level, spreading out for weeks — or longer — to render the land a sterile and useless area of reddish ash.

My two Allis Chalmers "crawler" tractors were required for the first ploughing. They usually worked as a pair in case one became bogged down. Special ploughs were used — a Canadian "Prairie Buster" or the Australian "Stump Jumper". The ploughing was followed by cultivators and harrows to pull out reed and other roots, which then had to be carted away for burning before the surface was rendered fit for sowing a crop. A smother crop came first before corn or roots could safely follow. The smother crop was often mustard, but for Rothschild's Thirty Acres it was too late in the year for this to be sown, and I decided on buckwheat. But that year of 1942 proved to be a wet summer and by October the buckwheat was still too green to cut. When November came it was a case of now or never, but not even the old-fashioned sail reaper was able to tackle the crop laid and tangled as it was. So with more cussedness than sense I decided to hand mow. Twelve of us mowed the whole thirty acres with scythes in three days and, knowing it would not dry out lying there, I had long narrow stacks made with air holes in the middle. When eventually it was threshed out, the resultant yield of seed was less than the cost of growing it.

Sid King had left in a huff and years later he sought me out to tell me that, with hindsight, he wished he'd stayed on. His replacement as foreman was George Long, a born fenman with four children of school age, who trudged daily the mile and a half to school in Burwell. As a village on the edge of the fens, it was itself a mile or more long, built on the sloping chalky uplands. Yet for all its length, the north end nearest to the fen and my farm was different from the upper, church end. The houses were smaller and many were sideways to the street with the old-time convenience of access to the fen by water. I'd hired a large three-storey barn which had obviously been used by some merchant or landowner, whose means of transport for whatever he dealt in or grew would have been by boat or barge. It was built of clunch, the local name for very hard chalk locally quarried, and many Burwell houses were built of the same material.

The difference between the north or fen end of the village and the church or upper end was in times past very marked, so far as people were concerned; the fen enders being more uncouth and sometimes aggressive enough to seek fights with the more genteel yeomen of the church or upper end. But such animosity was a thing of the past, even if the old could remember it as could those in Over. By contrast, Wicken village, from whence most of my helpers came, had no divisions of that kind. It was less than half the size of Burwell and much more compact, sited on a broad but low promontory of upland. To the north and beyond what was once a large mere, was Soham with its population of 5,000, larger than many market towns. But the size of a village was usually determined by the area and fertility of its surrounding land, and it was not until modern means of transport and cultivation, along with drainage, arrived that villages were made less distinctive through more widespread prosperity.

There was only one alternative to loading my sugar beet on to a barge provided by the Ely factory. This was by rail, which entailed carting the beet the three quarters of a mile up the main drove to where the hard road began. This was the site of both a brickworks and a fertiliser factory owned by Fisons, and was, in fact, the place where this large concern began way back. It originated with the discovery of a layer of fossils where the chalky uplands merged into fen, making it possible to dig through to its clay base. These fossils of marine life were mainly shells and were found to be rich in phosphates early in the nineteenth century and of value as a fertiliser, but by the end of the century it was no longer worth the laborious manual work. Fisons brickworks followed and a private railway was laid over the two miles to link up with the Newmarket-Ely line, and although we could order empty trucks for sugar beet, the drove was so soft in autumn and winter for heavy cart loads that iron shod wheels would often sink in up to their axes in black soup-like mud. A big improvement came in 1943 but until then it was seldom safe to drive even in a car down the drove to the farmstead in winter.

This access problem was especially difficult to overcome when stacks of corn needed to be threshed. I would have preferred to see the threshing machine powered by steam, but a ten-ton engine would have been in trouble from the start. The contractor sent his tractor for the job, but it often required both my crawler type tractors to move the heavy threshing drum to where it was due to work. Stacks of sheaves were placed for convenience in one or two central sites at harvest time for threshing in early spring. But once built, they had to be thatched and, for this job, an interesting character named Ted Edwards came from Burwell village on a piecework basis. A little man in his fifties, he had the rare ability to work and talk at the same time without slackening his pace.

"Did you ever hear of Edward's No-egg?" he asked me a few days after he'd begun.

His face lit up when I told him I recollected it being spoken of during the First War — how my father reckoned there could be no substitute for eggs in cake making.

"But there was — and it were my invention," he challenged. "I never let on what it was made of. And it sold well, time the war was on, but like a fool I kept on making it and got left with a big stock I couldn't sell, which ran away with all the profit I'd made. I'd have been well off if I'd not set up a factory in London in 1918, but I went bankrupt and come back to the land. You see, my father was a farmer and I knew how to thatch, so what with other jobs I can do on piecework I reckon I'm just as happy as I was when I were flush."

Although other Burwell men said it didn't do to expect Ted to tell the whole truth and nothing but the truth, I had no complaints about the speed and efficiency with which he thatched my twenty-odd corn stacks that autumn.

Skill and speed was not Bob Cranwell's strong point and because he had a chest complaint, I did not expect it of him. He was no more than forty and walked daily from Wicken except when off sick. He too was a talker, but preferred to ease off whatever light work he was on by asking questions of me and inviting my interest in his hobby of writing poetry and what he called "numbers". These, he explained, when I confessed to not knowing what kind of numbers he meant, were popular songs set to music. He longed to produce a "hit" but had failed to interest any agent to whom he submitted his "numbers". He had, however, an acknowledgement of a poem he had sent to the King. This poem was in very patriotic language and unlikely ever to be published, yet one had to show interest so as not to hurt his feelings. Bob's chronic complaint worsened and within a year or two a few of us went to Wicken to attend his funeral.

Billy Avey was another Wicken man who tried to foster his talent for music with song. His ambition was to compose both the words and tune of a national song in the belief that both the National Anthem and Land of Hope and Glory contained too much jingoism and belligerence. I could agree with this, but all he would tell me about it was that it required lots of skill and patience to reach the standard of orchestration he felt was essential, and that the first line was, "Oh England, my England, the land of the free". Billy was a tenant farmer under the post-1918 war County Council Scheme, but he had also a reputation as an agricultural engineer and it was in this connection that I sought his help. Before I became a farmer I'd heard how clay improved the black peaty soil. Some had already been clayed when labour was cheap and plentiful by digging holes in fields where clay was known to be the subsoil below the peat at a workable depth, to be spread around and ploughed in with the top twelve inches. One extra wide deep ditch had been dug by an excavator and out came enough clay to spread on to a strip some twenty yards wide, and when wheat was sown and harvested the yield from that strip was more than double that of the rest of the field. So I got the idea of making a machine which would dig holes to replace manpower.

I put my idea to Billy Avey and he agreed to take it on if I found him a place to work, and of course put up the money. Although I had no knowledge of engineering, I suggested a machine which would make trenches down to the clay and then heave up as much clay as possible for spreading before pushing the peaty overburden back in the trench. Billy said a better way would be to dig holes by means of a worm borer on the Archimedes principle, and this I had to accept. Having found a vacant shed in Wicken which was secluded, Billy began using acetyline welding. A year later his machine emerged, somewhat to the astonishment of a few Wicken folk, and was drawn down to the nearest field. It was a strange looking thing and it attracted the attention of Humphrey Jennings, who happened to be there shooting scenes for *A Diary for Timothy* under the Crown Film Unit in which I had been asked to play a part.

The claying machine began its trials with Billy full of confidence and me full of hope. It was tractor powered and began digging its first hole on a field which I believed held no more bog oaks. The boring worm went down, the peat came up to be pitched to one side, but at two feet there came a knocking shudder and a sudden stop. The blade was put into reverse, but only part of it came back to the surface for it had broken — proof that it had hit an oak which previous ploughing had not encountered. Billy said it could be repaired but the blade had been the most expensive and tedious part to make. I had to decline the offer but was left with a hankering notion that my trench digger would have been more suitable. This, Billy agreed to make, though protesting that his invention was soundest, in principle. In the event, when a few weeks later the new model was put to work I soon realised its fault. Not enough allowance had been made for the extra space required as the peaty soil came up on to a trough for pushing to one side of the trench. It would not move freely and its jamming made the whole machine seize up. Both machines stood idle until the sight of them as reminders of wasted thought, effort and money prompted me to ask a scrap dealer to take them away when my zeal for land reclamation for farm crops had begun to wane.

The incentive to become fully engaged with absorbing activities during the war years was not entirely due to the effects of the war itself. During the "phoney war period" of the 1939–40 winter it was clear that my efforts must be concentrated on maximum food production, especially as the demand for nursery grown plants had just about dried up. It was also for me a period of reassessment. Having largely achieved my ambition of making the Oakington nursery one of the largest for hardy plants in Britain, with thirty-six acres of stock in 1,800 kinds and thirty-six helpers, I began to think that I had been over ambitious and any sense of achievement now lacked substance. The profit motives had proved both fragile and illusory.

There were also personal complications in that my marriage had proved unstable to an increasing extent and for this I felt I must be partly to blame. It was all very well for me to do all in my power to save it, but the evidence had built up that I'd been at fault in some way right from the time of the proposal. We were simply not suited and the harder I tried to maintain the union, the more it seemed to widen the gap, and those who after five years had advised the necessity of children to bring stability were as far out as was I in believing this would be a cure for my wife's personality problems. And when the final break came in the summer of 1940, I felt devastated.

It was the period when there were very real fears of invasion but, having made sure that the three children all under six were well cared for, I felt a curious mixture of relief from a major source of stress with my wife no longer at home and in the care and responsibility of those more qualified than me. The feeling of having been let down was mixed with sadness, along with attempts to assess my future and a need perhaps to change my own priorities. Once the first priority of my children had been settled, I was at least able to cope easily with adapting the nursery to wartime needs and to go ahead with the farming and reclamation in Burwell Fen. But this entailed travelling twenty miles several times a week, and by mid 1941 I decided to move house.

Fordham was the native village of both my parents and, when they told me of a house there for sale, they suggested that if I bought it they would like to retire from their Mildenhall home and join me, leaving my brother George to take over at Mildenhall. Fordham was only three miles from Burwell and Brook House had over an acre of ground, intersected by a millstream — the river "Snail" — and so I did not hesitate. A new feeling of peace came over me. At Oakington I had been head Air Raid Warden. Here I had only one night a week on warden duty, and for the rest was able to sleep more soundly than I'd done for nearly two years.

The new environment soon brought new friendships and new incentives. At one time I even fancied I could take on another area of waste land to bring under cultivation, but wiser counsels prevailed. A boost also came when the King and Queen visited Burwell Fen to see the reclamation work in progress. This was on a part of the fen taken over by the "War Ag" near my farm, but my work was recognised by my being invited to join the Royal party. The bog oaks incidentally had been cleared but one was re-interred to show Their Majesties how they had lain. This encounter with its attendant publicity gave my ego something of a lift. And led to a request from my wife to return, as I'd said she could provided she had a genuine desire to fulfill her maternal role. But after two or three weeks, having been released from the Women's Army Corps on compassionate grounds, I came to believe she had not basically changed. This appeared to be confirmed by her willingness to agree to a legal separation with my having custody of the children.

During those years, home help was hard to come by, but even with a daily helper it was burdensome for my mother. My father helped as far as he could, loving the children as he did. But I had to agree to Bridget, the eldest, going to a boarding school at St Neots. Taking her there were sad times for us both for she was only eight years old. Robert and Adrian, her younger brothers, continued at a daily prep school in Newmarket, six miles away.

It had been a momentous soul searching decision for me — on the face of it I was denying the children their mother. I'd needed to convince myself that I was acting in their best interests and that my own were secondary, but in spite of not being fully satisfied at the time that I was being entirely impartial, in retrospect I can see it as the right decision.

For a few months my mother carried on as best she could with inadequate help. Advertising brought a few offers, but the one chosen was a forty-five-year old lady who set her sights on me rather than her duty as a nanny. Her stay ended abruptly after three weeks when Mother discovered she was a secret alcoholic. I advertised again in *The Lady* for a resident nanny and one of the few applicants was Myrah Holt who had a four-year old daughter. An agreement to come for a month's trial led to Myrah staying for twelve years. My mother, however, quite soon became suspicious of her. It was not just because Myrah had both good looks and a charming manner, but that by some means Mother learned that she was unmarried. Suspicions led to criticisms and when, after about a month, it became noticeable that there was a mutual attraction between Myrah and me, Mother could take no more and much to Father's regret they moved out.

But in my estimation, Myrah appeared to be the perfect substitute mother for the children, lacking nothing as a skilled and caring housewife. And when after a few weeks we both realized that we were deeply in love, it seemed that her needs and ours were fully met for a stable home life. Very soon news came that Bridget had gone down with measles at her boarding school. Complications set in and Myrah initiated her return home. Our doctor examined Bridget and diagnosed a threat of Bright's Disease. With his help and Myrah's exemplary care, she recovered fully with no more sad journeys back to school.

Myrah's tender care for the children was beyond reproach, but there were occasions when her attitude towards me was worrying. She sometimes became withdrawn and no amount of questioning or pleading on my part could break through — sometimes for several days. Then it would end suddenly as if it had been a purely personal matter for her. But finally the air cleared when she admitted that she had found it hard to be truthful about her marital status. I did not find it hard to believe whatever she told me, nor too difficult to forgive what had been deliberate lies. I was in love and wanted so much to make a success of what I rather glibly saw as a solution to my own, as well as my children's needs. What I failed to fully appreciate was that she saw her own situation as sometimes invidious. And because I was powerless to change it, her resentment sometimes surfaced in peculiar ways.

A Long Hop

For some of us imagination may lead to obsessions which tend to rule out alternative routes. As the war came to an end I decided to have done with the disappointments and lost labours of both Burwell Fen and Oakington as quickly as possible, to sell up and begin again well away from the area. The "War Ag" released me from tenancy of the 300 adjoining acres of Adventurers' Fen which I'd reclaimed but which was owned by the National Trust, and being in a hurry I sold the farm lock, stock and barrel for less than its true market value. As for the Oakington property, I'd had a good offer but the local District Council had clamped down forcing me to let them take it at a later valuation for their own development. The result was that I began the search for my ideal property with less capital than expected.

The search began in the autumn of 1945. I had a mental picture of a farm of up to 250 or 300 acres in a more hilly, wooded region, as a change from the rather flat, bleak lands of the fen country. I wanted a place with an ever-running brook or small river to use both for irrigation and as an amenity, having since childhood loved to manipulate water even in ruts or puddles. Going west appealed the most, but nothing was on offer that met my requirements except a valley farm on the Welsh border. An inspection was arranged but it never took place because news came of serious flooding there. December was scarcely a good time to view a distant property. Perhaps I should try again in the New Year over a wider area; take my time, making sure of getting just the right place, with the right kind of soil and at the right price.

At thirty-nine I was young enough to invest all I possessed so long as it was correctly placed, and with enough experience to ensure success whether I brought a farm or a nursery. But an orderly farm incapable of being improved, where there was no scope at all for "making two blades of grass where only one grew before", did not appeal to me at all. Several acres of scrub marsh would be an added enticement because its reclamation would be much more satisfying especially if, unlike Adventurers' Fen, I was the owner. A frosty spell with skating came to ease my fretting, but when that passed I took daytime trips eastwards into Norfolk and Suffolk just on the chance that my ideal might not be far away. And after all, I'd never studied and explored either county from the viewpoint I now hold.

Bressingham Hall was only the third farm for sale which I viewed. The house, at least from the outside, had instant appeal as a good example of Georgian architecture, set in a park-like meadow. The 228 acres included valley bottom land of the Upper Waveney river, and much of it offered abundant scope for reclamation and improvement.

"What about drainage?" I asked the owner.

He smiled wryly. "It's ironic," he said, "for years flooding has been a problem and now that I've decided to move, the Drainage Board are putting it right by deepening the river bed by three feet."

There were three kinds of soil. It was black and peaty in the valley bottom, much like that of the fen I knew. Up the gentle south-facing slope it was sandy loam, but becoming heavier above the main road which intersected the property — the A1066. With the assurance that the river was about to be deepened and with land suitable both for nursery and farm, I reckoned it was as near to my ideal as I'd ever find, for there were lots of mature trees as well. Some enhanced the eight-acre meadow between the house and the road and it made my imagination work again. Here, with fine oaks, elms and hollies was surely a perfect site for a large garden which would suit an enormous variety of plants, much wider than ever before, for the texture of the soil was just right — neither limey nor acid. All this with four tied cottages for helpers was on offer for £10,500. I took my young family to see it — my three and the housekeeper/nanny Myrah and her own daughter. All were excited and a week later I paid the deposit. The seven months' wait for possession at Michaelmas, 11 October, was hard to bear and slow to pass. Much needed to be done indoors to make the house more habitable, just as the land stood in need of improvement. But with unbounded enthusiasm I began the task even though I came across snags I'd overlooked.

The first snag was the weather. A wet harvest was followed by a cold, wet, autumn and a frosty December. Fields on to which I'd planned to move nursery stock from Oakington were so wet that plants had to be laid in, hopefully until spring. Then came what proved to be the most severe weather of the century. Frost lasted until mid-March 1947 and ended with a gale and heavy rainfall which caused the whole valley to be flooded. This delayed planting and upset other plans, and then by May a drought set in which continued for most of the summer. It seemed as if the dice was loaded against me, as if to show that I'd made too hasty a decision to buy the place. The promised deepening of the river by three feet was skimped so much that flooding would remain a hazard. Restrictions of one kind and another from still existing wartime stringencies compounded sheer bad luck from weather vagaries, to say nothing of my own miscalculations. Myrah complained about her invidious position as mistress, and I became disillusioned and depressed. Only the children seemed happy.

The end of a disastrous year brought to mind an urge I had had in my early twenties of emigrating to Canada. My imagination had been stirred by pioneering but I lacked then what it needed to take action. Now suddenly it flared up again to become another obsession. My mind very soon was made up and second thoughts were banished.

There were, however, obstacles both financial and logistic, as well as ensuring that what I'd begun at Bressingham would be carried on. I even convinced myself that a good manager might make more success of the farm and nursery than I could. I refuted my father's opinion that it was a foolhardy venture, and the thought of it being escapism was never in my mind. Nor did I stop to work out exactly the reasons for wanting to up sticks and go, being too much concerned with clearing away the hindrances. Myrah was all for it, seeing it as a way out of her position as mistress rather than nanny-cum-housekeeper. Both her daughter Philippa and my three children with their childish enthusiasm for adventure were in favour.

As a precaution against possible hard times I had all my pieces of antique furniture crated and sent on in advance. I also formed the business into a limited company, appointing an attorney to look after my affairs. He in turn appointed an experienced part-time overseer who chose a working manager and another man to be in charge of the office. Then, within a day or two of our departure, I had my first misgivings when the staff assembled to present me with an inscribed barometer and to wish me well. This invoked a feeling that I was perhaps running away and letting them down, but that feeling had to be pushed aside. I had already spent most of my financial reserve on fares and freight costs and there was no going back. Once we were aboard the veteran *Aquitania* at Southampton, forward-looking thoughts returned. I believed that the studies and contacts I'd made were reliable, just as I believed that British Columbia was the place to go, where freedom from restrictions of many kinds would enable me to be a family man with rosy prospects of success. Pioneering held a strong appeal for me as well as my belief that my children would find Canada a land of opportunity.

The luxury of first class travel and a smooth passage to Halifax, Nova Scotia was relaxing, but the twenty-six hour train journey to Montreal was very rough indeed.

Then came, for me at least, the thrill of five days and nights on the Canadian Pacific train to Vancouver which had always appealed to me. As we stood by our twenty-seven pieces of luggage we were met by the man with whom I'd been in contact as a go-between. He'd been very persuasive but, apart from making a hotel reservation, had done nothing about where to go from there. When he told me which hotel it was and what it would cost, I asked him to cancel it and I would find for myself a place I could afford. He walked off and we were on our own.

The rainy season had begun and our situation became increasingly stark as Myrah and I realised after enquiring at real estate agencies that we would need to search for a property without the children. They would, only temporarily we hoped, have to go to boarding schools, and I'd need not only to buy a vehicle but to pass a driving test. There was no option but to buy a van and put most of our baggage into the repository where the crated, advanced freighted furniture was already stored.

Heavy rain fell every other day as we went inland in search of a property. At first Myrah was uncomplaining. Having to cut costs by camping and frugality over meals soon brought tensions, but it was the noise of rain at night on the van roof which put her most on edge. When the terrain became more rugged and mountainous I decided to back-track on the south side of the Fraser river. I'd planned to seek a property in the Okanagon valley, and that was still over 200 miles away. But the properties for sale there were as uninviting as were those in the north — too large, too small, too sloping and all far more expensive than I'd been led to believe.

After two weeks of useless search we came back to Vancouver to make contact with the children before taking the ferry across to Vancouver Island. Landing at Nanaimo we obtained details of properties for sale. One was a few miles inland and only twenty dollars per acre, but it proved to be a large area recently logged off leaving an abomination of stumps and strippings. No house, no prospects. Further south there was a house on fifty acres of rocky outcrop, thin soil and a lake of forbidding appearance. The price was beyond my means, to Myrah's relief, because of its creepy atmosphere and dilapidated wooden house.

Other properties were inspected and left us with hopes sinking all the way to Victoria. On the way north again I made a tour on foot of a valley farm in need of drainage and went up to my waist in water when I tried to cross a ditch over a fallen tree trunk. That night Myrah was close to hysterics. Rain had made it impossible to cook supper on the Primus or to dry my clothes, and the loud patter of rain on the van roof became intolerable for her. But next day, in sunshine, there was one more call on my list.

It was just what we'd been looking for and the price of five thousand dollars was just within my reach. It was such a little for a well-built and cared-for house and twenty acres of which half was woodland, through which ran an attractive stream. When the affable owner asked for a deposit I offered a thousand dollars. He smiled quizzically and said it had to be five thousand since the selling price was fifty. I showed him the agent's paper. "Silly man — he knew what my figure was but has let us both down by putting only three zeros instead of four. Even at fifty thousand it's a snip." So once again we had to be on our depressing way.

There is — or was — only one road to take in order to travel from south to north on this 265-mile long island. Dejectedly we continued north on its pot-holed surface with no properties to view till past Nanaimo where we'd begun. But at Courtenay about seventy miles north I decided to go on further as darkness fell. It was now October and prospects were dismal. I had no option other than to go back to the mainland and try to find both a home and a job, a prospect which had no appeal whatever except on the score of hard necessity.

The van lights were just good enough for Myrah to spot a notice on a tree beside an opening in the forest. "Sea front house for sale". I braked, backed and headed down the narrow track for nearly a mile, and there it was — a low white building. An hour later I wrote out a cheque for fifteen hundred dollars as a deposit for a quarter of the price for six acres of recently logged-off land with the sea at the bottom of a steep slope. The owner had suffered a severe back injury and needed to go and live in Vancouver. We were made very welcome, almost as rescuers for the elderly Mr and Mrs Pocock in their plight, for they had not long since come here to retire.

Myrah and I slept that night in a bed for the first time for a month with the feeling that at last our luck had changed. Ten days later our crated furniture and the rest of our baggage in store arrived from Vancouver. The formidable task I knew it would be to clear and dig a garden patch would have to wait. Home-making came first, but to learn that there was no school so that the children could join us came as a bitter disappointment. Mont Pocock, the seller's brother, was neighbourly and helped me to build a shed for firewood from the furniture packing cases. Lack of dry firewood was the cause of much aggravation and what I sawed and split from dead or discarded trees smoked in the kitchen stove without giving out the heat Myrah needed for cooking.

And still it rained about every other day and channels had to be dug into a little creek from the logged off land to prevent the water reaching the house, which had piped water from a spring up the slope a hundred yards away. In mid-December the rain turned to snow and a frost set in.

Thoughts of the children coming back for Christmas were uppermost in both of our minds, and when the day came I drove the van over the rutty snow for fifty miles to Nanaimo, but only the girls came off the ferry. I'd not been told that the boys' school did not break till the following day and it was this second journey in a snowstorm, plunging off the centre into a snowdrift and a puncture, which ranks as one of the nastiest, most worrying journeys I have ever made.

But if Christmas was subdued and somewhat frugal, the children's joy lifted spirits for Myrah and me. As a couple we were drifting apart, for once they had returned to Vancouver our respective concerns, lack of comforts, home-making restrictions and the daunting outdoor work for me could not be shared or soothed. It was said to be the hardest winter for thirty years. The water supply froze, the flush lavatory failed and firewood became harder to find under the snow. Mont Pocock's water supply was dualled with ours and two weeks' hard labour was spent in tracing the frozen pipes and thawing them out. Then came the vital task of converting the rough terrain into a vegetable garden which involved drainage as well as clearance.

In March a large crate of plants arrived from Bressingham. I had ordered them to be sent as I had plans of working up stocks for sale. But about half of the sixty different kinds I unpacked were dead, due partly to inefficient packing and partly because they had been sent by sea via Panama, which meant five weeks from despatch to delivery. Money was running out, but when I was told that sock-eye salmon were fetching good prices I bought trolling lines and hired an ancient rowing boat. I rowed out to sea with a very nervous Myrah — a three mile wide passage between the islands. We got no salmon as a reward for five hours rowing, and trolling with oars I dare not strain over water said to be 800 feet deep. And next day the sight of a large school of killer whales where I'd been put an end to any wish to try again.

When I was told that a new island highway would pass not far away and that tall fence posts would be required, I decided to fell a dead cedar which the loggers had left alone as dangerous. Such trees were dubbed "widow makers", but though I worked alone

145

with a crosscut saw it came down without mishap and from it I split 120 ten-foot posts. A bouncing cheque for household supplies was the spur for me to ask the road contractors to buy the fence posts and give me the job. I found the overseer swearing at a gang of men trying to get a huge fire going where the forest was being cleared. He looked sourly at me and said, "No sale," as all fence posts required were already ordered.

"Any chance of a job then?" I asked.

He let drive at his helpers again before answering. Then with a scathing look he asked, "You're a Britisher, ain't you? Nope, I've never yet met a Britisher who could work."

I could but take this as a challenge and offered to prove myself saying, "If you'll take me on, I'll work for three days and you needn't pay me if you're still of the same opinion."

"Hell!" came his reply. "Nobody's ever said that to me before. And if it's piecework you want, you shall have it."

Over the next month I earned enough dollars with axe and saw, not only to relieve our immediate needs but for the next step of which I was becoming aware, based on the certainty that I could never make a realistic living out here in the sticks. The notion of pioneering was fast becoming an illusion. The sadness of not having the children with us was deepening, and I could feel sorry for Myrah even if relations between us had become strained. She too was disillusioned.

The children went back to boarding school after the Easter holiday with the assurance it would be the last term for them. A week or two later Myrah and I also travelled back to Vancouver and boarded the Canadian National train for the 2,500 mile journey to Toronto. In Ontario, I'd learned, properties in the farming districts were vastly cheaper than those on the west coast. And so it proved, for I was able to buy a house with one hundred acres for less than half of the price of the island property of six logged-off acres.

Half Way Home

It had taken nearly a month to find the place — at Cavan, twelve miles west of Peterborough, Ontario. I'd bought an old Nash car in Toronto, but once again had believed to my cost a seller's assurances which resulted in having to keep below 40 mph and pouring in up to a quart of oil every hundred miles to soothe the worn out bearings. We had chosen a Nash because its seats could be folded to make a bed for Myrah whilst I slept in a little tent every night. On this search, Myrah's phobia had centred on mosquitos which did not trouble me so much.

The four hundred or so miles of a circular route in southern Ontario included calls on a few nurseries in hopes of taking orders for Bressingham plants. But none came, nor was there any joy from a big firm who actually owed me money from a previous consignment. There was no usable road across Canada and the only way to drive back to the west coast was through America. The nursery at Newark in the adjoining state of New York rejected my request for payment because the debt was over seven years old and therefore no longer valid.

This maddening rejection of money I badly needed resulted in an anxious nine-day drive over nearly three thousand miles to Seattle. Motels and knife and fork meals were not for us, and I had but one American dollar left when we reached Seattle, and just enough Canadian dollars to pay for the ferry across to Victoria on Vancouver Island. It was now mid-June and with the children back we began packing. The furniture had to go by rail but the box truck ordered in which to pack it had been last used for coal. With Robert's help we brushed and shovelled coal dust away before loading it. We then used rope and nails to secure the furniture firmly and wood wool for the crockery and other breakables, in the belief that it would arrive at Cavan to coincide with our own arrival there in about ten days' time. We had no need for the Nash and the van now so they were taken away for scrap.

This third continental journey by steam-hauled train in less than a year was much less of a thrill, but our hopes of settling as a family were raised, especially when we found our neighbours had been tipped off and were there to welcome us. The owners of the house must have done this for Mrs Sissons had confided that she was on the point of leaving her husband if he delayed quitting any longer, whether or not the property had been sold. I'd paid only a deposit, relying on selling the island house quickly, but in the event it was not sold for nearly a year and they patiently waited several months for the rest.

We found it hard to be patient because the furniture we had sent in advance by rail did not arrive for nearly three weeks. And when it did, it was grimy with coal dust, and rough shunting or whatever had caused some damage. We were also tired of sleeping on bare floors and generally roughing it for lack of crockery and utensils. But no sooner were we reasonably comfortable again than another snag cropped up. The Sissons had assured us that the well on which the water supply depended had never failed in over forty years since it was dug. It was about fifteen feet deep with three feet of water when we arrived, but in drawing up two or three bucketfuls a day, after three weeks or less, there was only a foot and that came up discoloured with mud. Our conclusion was that the Sissons had managed on very little water indeed.

For the next few weeks I carried up buckets of water from a spring a hundred yards away down the slope, and not far from a big wooden barn with its heap of manure outside, which Bruce Sissons had been too tired to clear. The spring was only a trickle and in the hope of its being pure I dug a small collecting well lined with granite rocks which were abundant. The old well had been lined with them and when I went down to clear the mud at the bottom I was very conscious of the danger I was in as I squeezed down the ladder. To have dislodged only one could have brought down many more upon me as I worked at the bottom, and it was only family protests which made me desist. But my hopes of using the spring from which to draw water up to the house by means of an electric pump were dashed through a miscalculation of levels. Having first checked with a spirit level on a straight edge board over the uneven, rocky slope, I dug a trench believing it was just under the thirty feet maximum above which the pump would not suck. But after priming and trying several times, I checked again with the spirit level over the piping I'd laid nearly four feet deep only to find the lift, or fall to the spring, was thirty-two feet.

Between such tasks as hay making, burning down and filling in a stinking outdoor closet after purchasing an Elsan, I kept pretty busy. Then by way of a change I dug a ditch to drain a small swamp at the foot of the sloping arable fields. I dug test holes for water near the house but nothing but clay and rocks came out. I gave up on three sites at about six or eight feet, and then a man called to offer help. He was, he said, a water diviner and he had heard I was in trouble. Round he went with his forked stick and at one point down it went, only ten yards from the house. "Here it is!" he announced gleefully. "There's oodles of water right here if you've a mind to dig for it. Don't ask me how deep, but it's there okay, oodles of it."

This cheered me greatly on that Saturday evening after much hard labour in very hot weather, just after the meagre harvest had been gathered since only twenty acres of the farm was cropped. Next morning I began what I believed would be the final solution to the problem which had denied us the use of the bath and other toilet amenities during the very hot summer weather. I began digging within a five foot wide circle, throwing the spoil well back without much thought of how it would be cased in for permanency. Ten hours a day took me down to ten feet, but there was nothing but clay and a few glaciated rocks. At that point I had to make a platform so as to get the stuff on top in two stages, and I enlisted the help of Robert and Adrian to keep the spoil well back. At fifteen feet, a tripod and pulley was rigged up for me to fill buckets of clay — an empty one coming down as a full one went up for the boys to empty. A slip on Rob's part caused him to tumble and fall on top of me, flooring us both in the bottom. And then signs of the walls caving in spelt danger. The clay was now just moist enough to lose firmness and there were no means of shoring it at the then depth of twenty feet. From Peterborough I bought a "sand point" which, if driven into a water bearing stratum, would allow the pipe to fill without further digging and danger. To drive the thing down I used a heavy log on the pulley, but after two more days frustrating work I had to give up with the conclusion that for all his certainty the diviner had been wrong.

For the next few weeks, apart from helping neighbours who had helped me with muck carting, threshing and trying to please a cantankerous cow I'd bought for milking, I dug a trench three and a half feet deep and eight hundred feet long to a spring which one neighbour said I could tap. It was on his land and provided his own water, but the arrangement was to dig a new pipeline trench for him as well when mine was done. Devaluation of the pound in Britain had lowered my remittance from Bressingham and money was so tight that I had to take what casual work I could get. One job was to clear many years' deposit of hen manure from beneath a house in which a retired bachelor lived. It was a foul job, mostly on hands and knees, and in spite of him saying he would pay well for such a nasty job all he gave me was sixty cents an hour.

It was eighty cents an hour for the few days I helped to erect snow fences along local roads, but one offer of work I decided to refuse. It was to be grave digger for the district; not full time or year round, because frost from December till spring made such digging impossible, though it was safe to keep coffins in store. One other neighbourly job I had to refuse with some shame. It was to assist with killing and scraping a very large sow under primitive conditions. That was not long before Christmas, and by then water was at last on tap in the house with the long pipeline covered in to allow gravity to set it running freely.

Although one anxiety was over, others were building up. The children appeared happy enough that Christmas, but if Myrah still played her role as mother, there was neither outlet nor desire for intimacy between myself and her. And we were both troubled not only by lack of money, but because the local school was below standard. It was only half a mile for them to walk, but the one teacher had to cope with fifty children of various ages from five to fifteen. Only Bridget was old enough for High School and she went daily to Peterborough by bus. After Christmas I had to face up to stark realities. I'd not banked on making a living from the poor soil of the farm, but more on setting up a centre for exports of nursery stock from England. This idea I soon saw as merely wishful, along with the applications for a worthwhile job, all of which came to nothing. Nor was the Canadian press interested in any of the articles I typed out at night, and by day the Canadian winter was grimly in charge of all human activity outdoors.

In England I'd often longed for hard frost to bring me the joy of skating, but here it was scarcely considered, for more often than not the ice was covered deeply with snow. Only once was I able to skate, but being alone on strange ice in a strange land held no joy for me after the first few minutes in a temperature well below zero. What surprised me was how widely variable the temperature was. It sometimes went up or down by as much as 60°F in twenty-four hours and snow could fall as flakes, icy pellets or like sugar. But even if sometimes a brief rapid thaw took place, frost did not release its grip on the soil and this was why water pipes had to be three and a half feet deep.

Towards the end of January two disturbing letters came from Bressingham. Both were from staff members who reported that all was not well. My legal attorney had not long before reported that sales were disappointing and the bank account had gone into the red. But it was the bank manager himself who wrote to warn me that if I did not return soon there would be little or nothing to take over. The thought made me angry until it fully sank in that if those in charge at Bressingham were failing in their duty, I too was a failure. And because I also realised that I could never make good here in Canada, I had to go back and take up what I should never have left. It had been as my father had said, a foolhardy venture, an act of escapism which, if not conceived entirely for my own ends, was entirely my responsibility for pursuing so blindly.

It was not, however, just a matter of booking a passage back to England. This I did right away, but there had to be the sale of both the furniture and the electric cooker, fridge and washer which I'd acquired on h.p. as the money, or most of it, was needed to pay for the journey. The furniture was antique and an auctioneer was glad to take it — all except one very choice piece which I was obliged to sell locally for much less than its value. This was because the h.p. firm got wind of the move and sent in a bailiff who refused to leave until he had the money still owing. We felt sorry for him and made him comfortable overnight, and his stance changed when he knew that we were not out to cheat him. With nine hundred dollars in his pocket he left his deep footmarks in the snow.

We were a very subdued little party that left by train a few days later from Peterborough where we'd had to stay the night. It took most of two days to reach New York and on to the *Franconia*, second class. I filled an exercise book with the story of the venture, but when it was typed and submitted as a book the publishers turned it down because it made such depressing reading. Here I have been able to condense the story and view it with more detachment. From this distance in time some of the memories enable me to look back and laugh with hindsight, seeing how lacking I was in foresight.

I also look back and reflect how spartan my life was in most ways over that period of two years. The effect on Myrah and our relationship has been recorded, but the hardships affected her differently. At heart she was probably aware to a large extent that, but for her, I would never have taken such a radical step, though she must have been just as disillusioned as I was. But because she knew nothing of my inner secrets in a situation where masculine energy and resourcefulness were demanded in order to survive, those secrets had to be relegated with no opportunity of giving them the slightest outlet. Through that period and for some years after I tried to dismiss a softer side of my nature as rather despicable.

But with more privacy when I was back at Bressingham, the urge to give expression in a subdued way became too powerful to resist any longer. The self denial for what seemed a fear to be unconventional in such matters as wearing little gold earrings had to give way. But I had still a long way to go to understand and come to terms with whatever it was that made me feel an oddity and to live at peace with myself.

Diverse Doings

For a long time afterwards I looked back on the Canadian venture as an interlude which rid me of some false or faulty notions. To have got something out of one's system is much the same as admitting that it was a lesson I needed to learn. But it did not prevent other deviations I undertook as soon as economics allowed, all of which in some degree detracted from a single-minded approach to the business of running a farm and nursery for profit. I cannot pinpoint a single time or occurrence when striving for money lost much of its appeal. As a boy my siblings dubbed me a miser because I was so keen to save up pennies. Pennies from parents were usually for jobs performed and once having saved eleven, I stole one from the shop till to make it into a shilling, and within an hour or two put it back as guilt prevailed. When I was about twelve years old I won several races and jumps in the Church Sunday School sports. This brought me the wealth of about two shillings, but the look on the faces of some of the losers prompted me to share it with them, which made me feel good even though at the time I was keen to show off boyish strength and skill.

The 1930s were a period of growing prosperity in business but when war came with the virtual collapse of profitability as well as of my first marriage, my self confidence was somewhat undermined with thoughts that a one-track mind lacked reliability. I could not bring myself to take advantage to any extent of personal gain from my wartime activities. In the event, what increase there was in my finances was lost in the Canadian venture, but once that loss had been made good back at Bressingham, then came the urge again to work, not so much for profit as for what could be termed a kind of self expression.

This for me meant not only being dedicated to the land, to care for its fertility, and for what it would grow, but for its potential amenities as well. In a burst of enthusiasm I planted hundreds of trees. These were mainly Canadian poplars (Robusta) but I also scoured the woods for seedling ash, oak and alder, as well as having choked up ditches dug out. During winter months it was a pleasure to wander with spade and axe to improve drainage or sever the hold which ivy had on trees, as well as to plant more trees. If sometimes my conscience pricked for not spending more time with my children, I compromised to some extent, but felt most of the time they needed to develop their own ideas and become self reliant. What was a kind of recreation for me would be tiresome work for them and I soon gave up asking them to help with nursery work, in which the two boys showed no interest whatever during their school years.

I should explain that the valley bottom was known as Bressingham Fen. It was almost all on the northern flank of the infant River Waveney, which served also as the boundary between Suffolk and Norfolk. The fen area, no more than half a mile wide had been carved up into fields by ditches and some shelter belts probably in the early 1800s. Less than a quarter of this hundred acres had been used even after the 1940s drive for more productive land usage. The rest had reverted to woods or marshy scrub, of value only for so-called sporting with guns. Indeed, the sale brochure had described it as a small "gentleman's sporting estate".

My attempts to bring more of it under cultivation in 1947–8 had only partially succeeded, with twenty acres of scrub being cleared and sown down to pasture and crops. But poor drainage was a recurring handicap both to arable crops and nursery stock, although when not waterlogged the land was easy to work. But when farm crops failed and when, as happened more than once, nursery plantings had to be rescued from drowning and even from beneath ice, it was somewhat disheartening. It was a hazard which culminated in the most disastrous flood of all in August 1987.

Although I have always been keenly aware that had I been more thorough when searching for the ideal farm in 1946, I would never have settled on Bressingham, there was always some hope that the flooding problem would be cured by improving the river outfall lower down stream. Since the 1987 flood the offending reach has been dredged, but it still needs another very rainy spell as proof.

Grim reminders of my hasty purchase of Bressingham Hall farm have often occurred, but luck was on my side when I chose the dry summers of 1955 and 1959 to dig out the two-acre lake. Modern equipment would have done the job in less than half what it took us with our rear scoop tractor. It might have been cheaper, but I did not count the cost of my own labour and the help that Robert and Adrian gave — then in their middle teens.

The lake was by way of a consolation for the lack of amenity water at Bressingham, but it also served to improve the two adjoining fen fields when some 10,000 cubic yards of sandy clay were mixed in with the peaty soil. And it was much more rewarding than the pond I made at Oakington in 1937 when only hand labour and barrows were used.

There is no point in counting the monetary cost of such projects. The labour and the cost becomes quite immaterial when a job is done to fill a deep-seated yearning. I believed the two-acre lake would be a permanent amenity, and hopes of its aesthetic value quickly materialised because it fitted in with the landscape and now gives the appearance of having always been there. And over the years I've often found peace and solace using the punt I had made, as well as pleasure when the ice is strong enough for skating.

Reflections on punting and skating take me back again to the late 1920s and 1930s. Whenever I had the opportunity I most enjoyed being on the Ouse at Over for both fishing or simply to be alone, close to nature, with renewed peace of mind. In winter when the floods were over hundreds of acres I used a gunning punt which could be hauled over banks if need be. Ostensibly I was after flighting duck, but found it thrilling to pit my strength and wits against wind and water with only a pale moonlight for guidance and through gaps in fences and hedges, admitting to myself what a crazy kind of enjoyment it was.

My craze for speed skating was of much the same order. In trying to live up to the reputation I had, to be the first on and last off the ice, sometimes led to mishaps. On more than one occasion the ice gave way. If it was only my legs that got wet I carried on in the belief that no harm would result if I kept on the move. But once I went in up to my waist and with skates off on dry land I lit a fire, took off my wet clothing and donned an overcoat to cover naked parts until the fire dried my clothing enough to put on again. During a three-week frost in 1929 I skated all day and every day, entering races but never winning one. When it ended, a backlog of work had to be done and the net result was yellow jaundice which depleted my energies for a year or more.

Abundant energy has not always been an unqualified blessing for me. When applied to notions which were either half-baked or wrongly conceived, the energy I used up was virtually a waste of effort. In such cases I had to learn the hard way — coming to see the job from a more sensible angle. One of my failings, however, has been the inability or the cussedness of failing to learn how to take a sober or sideways, calculating view of each new idea or project which came to mind. Sometimes obvious snags were sufficiently deterring, but sometimes they merely heightened the challenge, especially when my own labour was involved. The tougher the task, the greater the satisfaction on completion, but with the passing of time both the successes and failures have lost significance. A few linger as amusing memories. I also reflect on how my brothers' and sister's careers turned out to take on unconventional aspects.

Eric, my elder brother, was the only one not to inhabit Meadow House at Oakington. He had drifted somewhat with no acceptable bent on leaving school. The then still current belief was that the cure for indolence or intransigence was to be sent to the colonies, and at nineteen he was shipped off to Australia. He returned, as it happened, just in time to see the start of the 1934 air race to Australia from Mildenhall where my parents were then living. He settled finally to become an entertainer, with magic and puppetry his special gift, amusing mainly children and old folk with considerable success. But had he been given the opportunity to develop at an early age I'm pretty certain that some wider talents would have emerged.

Perhaps the same remark could be applicable to myself — and to my sister and younger brother. The latter became a very efficient nurseryman for glasshouse crops as he took over the Mildenhall nursery. His main hobby became racing, first as a motor cyclist and then on to go-carts and he became British Champion in his fifties. Kay (Kathleen) was a somewhat reclusive artist, never to marry, and never ambitious. As for me, three New Testament quotations often come to mind. One is the Parable of the Talents, and in retrospect I realise how I failed to live fully up to its message. The second one is "What shall it profit a man to gain the whole world but lose his own soul?" This was a warning, but there was some contradiction between the two and I seemed to oscillate between them as I also tried to live up to St Paul's advice, "Whatsoever thy hand finds to do, do it with thy might". Much as I believed the truth of the first two, it was the third which had the greatest appeal throughout my life, having no shortage of energy and the incentive to practise it.

Some digressions are difficult to avoid in this type of book, in which the jumbled facets of my life resist orderly classification. The biblical quotations above were read and digested from Sunday School days when I was a choir boy much influenced by Church of England doctrines, traditions, stability and sanctity. It was not until I reached my later teens that doubts and criticisms began to creep into my mind. In reading a variety of books over the years I became more and more aware of my own ambivalence, of wanting to shed the kind of Christianity on which I'd been reared, in favour of a more humanistic or agnostic approach, but at the same time seeking for a reliable faith by which to live. This desultory seeking and the relative peace of mind which came after returning from Canada led me to the simple, yet deep and uninhibited beliefs and practices of the Quakers. After attending several of their meetings I became a Member of the Religious Society of Friends (to give their correct title) in 1951.

In fact, I'd had pacifist leanings for several years previously and during the invasion threat of 1940, but feared I might not have the courage to act in keeping with them if for example enemy soldiers threatened my children in some way. Such fears I kept to myself, but on one occasion at a social gathering I caused offence by saying that much as I hated what the Germans were doing, I could not hate them as individuals, deluded as they were. At the time I was head Air Raid Warden for the village which adjoined an RAF bomber station, with a siren on the house chimney to set off when telephoned warnings came.

In 1952 I took a holiday, partly on business, to Germany, Austria and Switzerland, with only a rucksack as baggage. The combined effect of changed circumstances and Quaker membership made me feel more free and open-minded than I had since boyhood, which allowed a reversion to childhood openness. On that two week trip I made contact with Quakers in Cologne and Munich and had many a talk with people who responded to my question — "Do you speak English?", but I was snubbed when I asked a Catholic dignitary in Innsbruck if he knew of a Quaker centre there. A friendship which has lasted ever since was made with a nurseryman near Darmstadt and he it was who invited me to be a judge at a large horticultural show in Hamburg the following year, which I did not enjoy. Moving on to Denmark on business my propensity for asking people "Do you speak English?" led to a one-off break from several years of celibacy in Odense.

With business completed, I went on to Oslo and boarded an early morning steam-hauled train en route for Bergen. As planned, I left it at a mountain station to follow a marked trail so as to walk the twenty-five miles or so to another station and on to Bergen. I walked for three hours uphill into the most rugged terrain I'd ever traversed without seeing a soul. The higher I went, the more conscious I was of a peculiar feeling of being utterly alone but in tune with the world of nature. Not that there was any wild life other than what little could grow in such inhospitable conditions, probably under snow for much of the year. The wind was keen, the clouds dark and squally. Quite suddenly it began to rain and I hurried on to a cluster of huge rocks ahead for shelter. Standing close to one almost as big as a house, I pondered over how even this could support lichen and was gradually overcome with a sense of awe and wonder, which made me feel at first very insignificant indeed. A lump came to my throat and then for I don't know how long I was convulsed with sobbing. All my strivings, my ambitions, my self-esteem, my hopes and fears became submerged in the overwhelming sense of being simply a minute but integral part of the whole realm of nature in an almost cosmic sense.

As a revelation and the most profound emotional experience I'd ever had, I could not see or feel that God was directly involved. At the age of forty-seven my hazy notion of God was still that of a supreme personage as taught by organised Christianity, but I could see no connection or divine intervention. The only message I was able to glean from the experience was to be less self-centred and to practise much more humility. I wanted to write down some thoughts and impressions without delay lest I forget, but standing there and beginning to shiver I moved on somewhat dazed, with several miles to go to a mountain hostel near Finse where I was to stay the night. Later, I did record my impressions but it took many years of thinking, seeking and learning before concluding that

God is a spirit beyond comprehension and not almighty in the accepted doctorinal sense, and that we humans are merely the most evolved of species, charged with expressing and working with the Divine Spirit to the best of our ability as individuals. In such a context the three biblical quotations earlier in this chapter certainly had a place — at any rate for me.

Unsought Fame

It has now become clearer that much of what is recorded in the last chapter was an important factor in my gradual edging away from striving solely for profit. Yet the nursery business was expanding and the main purpose of my visit to Denmark was to clinch the purchase of new plants raised there. I had put off garden-making during the first three years after the Canadian interlude but by 1953 the urge to begin became too strong to resist any longer. On the west side of the house I made a pool flanked by raised beds for alpines. Then came the island beds for perennials in the large unkempt lawn on the north side, nine beds of informal shapes to fit in with a curving shelter belt. These, as I have already explained elsewhere, were experimental, in the belief that they would overcome the faults inherent in the conventional one-sided herbaceous border.

There were of course quite valid excuses for making these nine island beds, including my wish to see perennials in wide variety growing in groups as a change from nursery rows, with the added pleasure of arranging them for decorative effect. As for enlarging a horse pond into a lake the following year, there was only the lame and quite invalid reason that it would serve as a reservoir for irrigation. With the mental picture of what I wanted it to look like when it was finished, the sweaty labour it involved was almost a pleasure in itself.

By the following spring of 1956 the somewhat panhandle-shaped pond filling the low side of a seven-acre field had already been used for skating. With some water lilies, reeds and other plants established and a few flanking willows, and of course stocked with fish, I was very content. Contentment, however, applied only to my work and the relationship with my three children. Relations with Myrah Holt had never recovered and she had become withdrawn and cold, especially towards me. Not that this was one-sided, because it had been obvious that we were now incompatible. She did her job as housekeeper, but when my three admitted to a lack of respect or affection towards her, I hoped she would decide to leave. I lacked what it would take to tell her to go after eleven years, especially as her daughter Philippa had accepted me as substitute father. Then, quite unexpectedly, I gained my freedom to marry again after sixteen years. Myrah packed up and left with a modest golden handshake from me, which left me somewhat skint. Much relief from the long standing tension between us followed, but I could but feel sorry for her. We had been lovers; she had both good looks and charm when she felt able to use them, as well as several talents. Yet she had missed out on so much in life and now at forty had, so far as I could tell, a bleak future. I never saw her again but learned a year or two later that she had married and gone to California. She was never heard from, or of, again, not even by Philippa who vainly asked the Salvation Army to trace her. Incidentally, Philippa developed epilepsy in her teens and Flora, my new wife whom I married after six weeks' acquaintance, gave her refuge for a time.

I regarded my second marriage as a second chance. Being conscious that I must have failed in various ways as a husband previously, I made a full confession and adapted as best I knew how in spite of being twenty-three years older than Flora. There was much that we appeared to have in common. I gladly gave up some of the self-sufficient bachelor habits into which years of celibacy had tended to push me, and tried to live up to the ideals which I appeared to represent for Flora. She was wholehearted, and proud of her Yorkshire-bred ability of being undevious in every way.

Yet, in spite of our appearing to have so much in common in our ideas and ideals, some misgivings crept in at a deep level after a time. These seemed to be a fear that I might not be able to reach her estimation of the kind of man I was, with her belief that I was her ideal despite being so much her senior in age. Because she had fitted in so well from the first, with my offspring being all in favour of her taking on a central role, I tried hard to play my full part. Yet this niggling anxiety persisted and after only a few years this became a threat. It sparked off a need to become absorbed in another project; one which had long been shelved for lack of time and incentive.

The time and work in forming the Hardy Plant Society was absorbing. But once it was off the ground with my election as its first chairman, Flora took on the job as temporary treasurer, dealing with over seven hundred members in the first year. Whatever she did was done unstintingly and, when in the autumn of 1957 I began extending the garden, she was all in favour of it. We visited other gardens, met old friends and made new ones, swopping whenever new acquisitions were available, for which Flora wrote the permanent labels. Although she did no garden work, she was fully supportive, curtailed only when two girls, Anthea and Jenny arrived in the early 1960s.

By 1962 the number of island beds had reached forty-seven, covering five acres of the meadow apart from the grassy walks and tree girt surrounds. And the number of different species and cultivars increased to about 5,000 to make it the most comprehensive collection of hardy perennials in the country. Garden making included wall-building and with no suitable bricks available I decided to use flint stones. These I selected from heaps of rejects available at gravel pits some distance away. Through trial and error I found a way to make them presentable where walls were needed to terrace slopes or make raised beds for alpines. As a solitary occupation it was both fascinating and relaxing at odd times when free of the demands of the nursery business, then with close to one hundred helpers. But with garden making complete I then felt a need for some other all-absorbing interest.

The only resentment I nursed now and then over these post-Canada years was the wanton destruction of *Bella*, my first traction engine. Early in 1961 it erupted into a decision to buy another now that my writing efforts were bringing in a little money. I'd heard that steam nostalgia was pushing up values of those engines which so far had escaped the scrap dealers' clutches, and I was able to buy one in good order for £180. Its arrival and to put it in steam gave me enormous pleasure, because ever since I could remember these cumbersome old-timers had fascinated me. The excuse I'd had for paying £50 for the one which was cut up whilst I was in Canada was to use it for clearing scrub and sawing wood, but this engine was mine, as a pet or hobby, pure and simple.

From the first some people who came to visit the garden on Open Sundays showed interest in *Bertha*. This gave me an excuse to put her in steam and then to give short rides on the fuel bunker, which was as much a pleasure for me as for the children who eagerly clambered up while their parents watched. Very soon I was searching for others, for it was plain enough that nostalgia for steam was very real and that would send up the value of the dwindling remnants of the steam age. By the end of that year there were eight in various stages of dereliction in the yard. During that winter, with voluntary help, almost every evening was spent in a draughty barn scraping rust and cleaning down to bare metal with my mind somewhat agog. It had become another obsession. Its possibilities were somewhat beyond my ken, but the hunch came with increasing conviction that more engines would bring more visitors to Bressingham and so increase the gate money I enjoyed giving to charities.

There is no need to record in detail how the first engine in 1961 led to a total of forty on wheels for both road and rail by 1972. In this book it is motivations rather than locomotives that matter. During that period I seldom paused to reflect on what my motives were. I could not see far beyond the opportunities which occurred to acquire more as the larger concept of a comprehensive live steam museum unfolded. Some of the early arrivals of the fourteen road-using engines were so rusty and decrepit that some of my family expressed fears that I'd gone crazy. They were sceptical when I protested that they would prove to be a good investment. This was with tongue in cheek because I knew I would never sell them unless forced to do so, and when in 1968 the first railway locomotives were offered to me, I set about applying for charitable status as a museum.

Robert and Adrian had both been away for a few years but came back for good in 1962. Both were keen to expand the business, but by the time I handed over control of it to them in 1970 the necessary locomotive shed of 13,000 square feet had been built. I was much more convinced than they were that one way and another the steam museum would be an enhancement overall, diverse though it was from a nursery business. I'd had opposition to overcome by degrees to narrow gauge tracks being laid, so felt it was up to me to do most of it myself with help from the small, separate museum staff. It was the kind of work I relished anyway, making track beds and laying sleepers to carry the rail. All the work and materials had to be on the cheap whenever possible, to avoid cost and inconvenience to the nursery. I should mention that the little railways brought income for the first time which did not go to charities but to meet expenses, including restoration costs and wages.

The day when I gave up opening the mail, with Robert and Adrian replacing me as Managing Director of Blooms Nurseries Ltd, arrived in 1970. Although no more than sixty-three years old, I'd had about forty years as the boss and it was time to let my sons go ahead without my clamping down on their initiative. Expansion was in their minds, whereas I was inclined to consolidate, not wishing even to go in for container grown plants — the demand for which was growing with the spread and popularity of garden centres. Nor had I any desire to depart from being wholesale only, which was simpler and less exacting. At heart I realised I was being cussed and not very realistic because not only was the nursery trade changing from both production and sales traditions, but our retailing customers were reluctant to stock and sell the many new or uncommon kinds we grew and offered for distribution. A small retail section was begun in 1964 and was steadily growing by 1970, as was the range of conifers, heathers and shrubby subjects which were Adrian's speciality. It was clear that both my sons were now firmly wedded to the nursery business and needed my sanction to forge ahead. My misgivings on the dubious wisdom of rapid expansion were expressed, but I felt I had no right to be obstructive.

I could not, of course, delude myself that my efforts to set up a comprehensive live steam museum hampered to some extent my devotion to the business and to the new garden. Work such as track laying was my job in relatively slack periods, and taking on separate paid helpers for engineering and restoration tasks had to a large extent allowed me time for planting and propagating of the special kinds of plants I grew for the nursery on land near my house. These were new or rare subjects for which hand work was safer than the more mechanised nursery methods of potting and planting. There were about 400 different kinds which occupied four acres. My early retirement, therefore, was by no means a case of taking it easy, but of giving me more time for what I preferred to do, whilst giving my sons the power to do likewise. With my enthusiasm and energy still unflagging, the thought of taking it easy was anathema to me as was Flora's suggestion of moving away to retire properly, with just enough garden to keep me healthily occupied. My refusal, though not harshly given, served to deepen the widening rift between us which neither of us possessed the ability to bridge, and it was only our love for our two children Anthea and Jenny that held the partnership together. Even then the holidays we took with them were for the most part linked to my obsessive interests in some way, apart from a few package trips abroad.

The dozen or so years in which the steam museum was developed was in a way the most exciting period of my life. It added an entirely new dimension to both my thoughts and activities with problems — logistic, legal, family and financial — to be overcome, and yet it was the conjugal rift which most often recurred and was the most intractable. Sometimes the inner conflict which this problem engendered was so intense that sleep became elusive. Sometimes a kind of mental and physical seize-up occurred, forcing me to stop worrying whether or not I was fundamentally at fault. For two or three days I had to avoid people and whenever possible work alone, out of the way — or just slink away to be alone. Then came gradually a renewal, not only of energy and zest but of a conviction that I could not and must not change course — that if I were to give up striving for what I believed was very worthwhile I would regret it for the rest of my life.

It was during this period that inklings first came that there was not only a creative element in my form of gardening and the steam museum endeavour, but that the impulse and incentive might be a form of sublimation. At the time I'd merely seen this as a possibility, but tracking down the underlying cause was beyond me. Attempts to do so were confusing, but there was surely some possible link between my past and present obsessive projects and the somewhat psychological ambiguities of my nature, which I'd tried to suppress with not much success for lack of knowledge and understanding.

The year 1970, when I was sixty-three, was the most traumatic of my whole life, and at times I was afraid I might even go round the bend. I consulted a psychiatrist, but after three sessions the advice he finally gave was merely a reminder that I alone must be responsible for any decisions I made. What stood out starkly for me was the need to understand and come to terms with myself, to read the kind of books which might shed a light on my ambiguities and peculiarities. They had proved much too basic and powerful to be overcome by a willpower which itself was ambivalent.

This account must not lapse into one in which the emphasis is on self justification. I'd already had cause to doubt my own motivations and integrity, especially in so often having convinced myself that what I wanted to do was the right course to pursue wholeheartedly. Also that I'd not stopped to think of others whom I might be manipulating or taking unfair advantage of. A recurring subject of contention had centred on the increasing number of visitors. It spanned the garden-making periods and became even more of an issue with the growth of the steam museum. Open Days to the public between 1960 and 1970 had increased from once a month in summer to twice a week from Easter to early October. The loss or restriction of privacy was worthwhile to me, but others of the family voiced some criticisms — with the hint that I was guilty of self aggrandisement. But however much I dug down trying to discover my basic motivation, I could never get beyond the fact that visitors enjoyed coming to share the pleasure it had given me to provide the means. Such sharing was the basis of my incentive and I felt justified in overriding objections.

Up until 1968 I'd taken pleasure also in giving the gate money to charitable causes at the end of each season. The volunteers for gate duty represented some of these and received their share, and over the ten years of well spaced openings a total of £33,000 had been dispensed.

As a family we were none of us at all well off, and perhaps I should have been more responsive to their "Charity begins at home" suggestions. In the event all this went sour, for not having been warned that in the circumstances the gate money was taxable, the tax men pounced when I decided the steam museum should become an independent Charitable Trust. The final outcome was a demand for £12,000 back tax plus £9,000 or so for expenses due to the accountants handling the case with the Revenue Inspectorate over a period of several years. In spite of such setbacks, this one having been overcome by my giving all my personally-owned traction engines to the Trust, the museum became firmly established entirely upon people paying to see steam in action and the garden. It could not have expanded but for that and for the skilled and devoted staff I've been fortunate enough to employ — having now reached eighteen full time people. Open Days now attract 120 to 150,000 visitors every year from far and wide, and the total value of the exhibits has risen enormously. But it never occurs to me that it is an achievement of which to feel proud, any more than does the garden. For one thing I had willing helpers; for another, further improvements are needed, and my own work involvement was such an absorbing pleasure that it was more like an end in itself. Genuine, unalloyed pride of achievement can be justified only when the objective is complete and faultless. None of my endeavours have ever reached that peak, nor can I imagine will ever do so.

Coming to Terms

At eighty-eight time is fast running out for me. It is always later than you think, and the older I become the most swiftly the years seem to pass. Even so, with much I would still like to do and learn I tend to look ahead rather than over the years gone by. What hits back at me rather forcibly is that so many essentials of what one needs to know in order to live fully were not learned until I turned seventy. I can see now that I should have begun to learn them at seventeen, but at that age my ignorance of the facts and factors of life were abysmal. Such knowledge might not have prevented me from becoming somewhat eccentric or a maverick, but would surely have enabled me to make wiser, wider choices and so avoid inner conflicts and hurts to other people, as well as many a blunder.

At seventeen I was gauche, gullible, and opinionated but open natured enough to be noticed as having potential. I was aware of the latter to the extent of believing that it would develop more or less automatically, even if I had no grandiose ambitions at the time beyond that of becoming a leading nurseryman. The future for me was in my mind, but to some extent I was reclusive with a lively source of fantasies to call upon. These included notions of the kind of woman I would choose for a wife and the reward this would be to match her essential virginity with my own. I believed in the sanctity of marriage and the sinfulness of fornication. At the time I didn't know the full meaning of such words and several others relating to sex, nor did I know exactly how babies were conceived. I once asked Father the meaning of the word rape. His faltering reply was, "What the Germans did to Belgian women". This left me guessing but its full meaning did not come until years later, leaving me sorry that Father's reticence had also been so inculcated when young. I'd never been told and knew of no informative books, and what little I did know came from one or two talkative men at work.

My fantasies were much more appealing and romantic, but sometimes they took a strangely different shape or course, as if there was a feminine element somewhere inside me in need of recognition and expression despite the rugged masculinity I tried and wanted to display. Attempts to squash such unnatural, unworthy thoughts as being sinful did not banish them for long. Nor did it ease my puzzled mind to reflect that my earliest memory was of wanting to be a girl. It dimly occurred to me at the time when living in lodgings at Tunbridge Wells that a girl friend was the answer. It needed courage but having met one willing to take a country walk on a Sunday afternoon and another to treat to the cinema and fish and chips, there were no further incentives to form a friendship. I hadn't enjoyed their company and I doubted if they had enjoyed mine. So it was back to solitary rambles and bike rides with my fantasies, ambitions and unsatisfied longings.

There was no one in whom I dare confide. I could not imagine that a book existed which would tell me what I wanted to know. Nor did I realise how little I knew of human nature, including my own. When musing, if some lack of understanding occurred, I would mostly dismiss it as unimportant. For example it suddenly appeared odd that males also had nipples, which could never serve the purpose of suckling babies as did women's. Why then did God, who created Adam as the first human, include nipples? Not having come to see the creation story in Genesis as allegory, I could but conclude that after making Adam complete he later changed his mind, making Eve as an afterthought as the helpmeet to Adam and the bearer of children. It was not until I began to remedy my ignorance years later that I learned that the female came first in sex evolutionary biology.

I cannot but regret the waste and the lack of incentive for learning during those years of ignorance. The means to study were not really available, but the fact was that I was unaware of how little I knew about life with a capital L outside the confines of the village and its social narrowness, coupled with the hold which Anglican doctrines still held over me. And it was not until war came in 1939 that the shake-up and shake-out began for me — together with a marriage break-up. For twenty years my reading had been confined mainly to history and travel with occasional dips into theology by popular writers such as Leslie Weatherhead, Donald Soper and C. S. Lewis. All stirring stuff, but their effect on me was transient and superficial. Later on the writings of William Temple and Teilhard de Chardin were too deep for me to fully grasp. None shed any light on my quirkish secret nature, all evidence of which I had managed to hide or suppress. It was not until I was forty-eight that a Harley Street psychiatrist explained that what had been troubling me was not confined to me as I'd imagined it was. But apart from saying I should not feel guilt and shame and that I'd learned how to live with it quite well, he gave no hint of its origin.

The first book I read which threw some light on the conundrum was Simone de Beauvoir's Second Sex. Although so much of this massive treatise deals with the degradation of women in a man's world, it had a message here and there for me and shed some light on my ambiguity and ignorance. These revelations led quickly to delving into a wider range of books on the psychology of sex, gender and what not. Some by American authors were of no more than superficial value. Not so Carl Jung's researches and beliefs, but these were less easy to digest than were two paperbacks by two English women. The Descent of Woman by Elaine Morgan and The Spirit of the Valley by Sukie Colegrave were for me especially revealing and thought provoking. A book which seemed to hold the final answer was Androgyny by Jean Singer. Having read these three books again, I believed I'd found the answer to my problem. I'd also reached my three score and ten years of age. The sum total of what I have gleaned from these has made little difference to my way of life, but has at least softened me as a person because at last I have come to terms with myself through understanding and acceptance.

To know that we are accepted by other people "warts an' all", gives not only a warmth of feeling but a continuing desire to live up to that image, though we may never be able to see ourselves quite as others see us. Even less likely are we to be the kind of person at heart which others imagine we are, but acceptance of what from deep searchings we come to terms with ourselves does at least give a surer footing. Some people, myself included, have to admit or accept that we are in some degree eccentric. We are in conflict with ourselves if we try to be as normal as are the majority. A steam engine will not work without eccentric valves which at first sight appear to be in opposition to the general thrust of power. Human eccentrics, when evidence of abnormality shows, are dubbed as cussed, quirky or maverick. But as hang-ups of many kinds are likely to be secret whims or indulgencies, relatively few of us become exposed as eccentrics.

Learning from books about the much neglected subject of human nature prompted me to give in to two very long-standing urges — of wearing long hair and earrings. These urges had been constant from early childhood and having reached an age when I cared much less what people thought, I indulged and gained considerable relief and satisfaction. What I'd read convinced me that to have a feminine streak in my basic make-up in no way detracted from the masculine. Sex and gender are separate factors and conjectures on my part are of little or no value. What matters most is that release and relief have at last come and allowed not only a more peaceful mind, but an influx of goodwill such as I'd never known before towards other people. Albeit slowly, the barriers I'd felt obliged to build around myself began to crumble as a warmer, softer attitude towards others seeped in.

Before I came to see myself as fully male but with an implanted element of the feminine in my make-up, I found considerable relief in joining the Beaumont Society. But it was not after all for me. I had no desire to pretend to be a woman by dressing up as such. Although a need in longing to give some expression to my Yin-Yang nature was constant, there had been long periods in my life when suppression of the Yin brought out the more aggressive dominating masculinity. It was during these periods that I made the greatest blunders and caused the most hurts, especially to women. None of them knew just what I was suppressing, nor did I intend to hurt them. Over the years a few women have appeared to see me as macho or charismatic and there has been evidence of this even since I became old — far more in fact than when young.

I have found it much easier to be more extrovert now that I've broken down the reserve or shyness towards women which bothered me greatly when younger. Since I came to terms with myself, I have made friends with several women who showed some interest or friendliness towards me. Most of them were of mature age and a few lecturing trips to America led to more letter writing afterwards, with confidences sometimes exchanged. All were however strictly platonic, as are more recent friendships, if only because my record is not good in the few cases where full intimacy had come about. To some extent the adage "In youth denied the means; in age denied the power" is applicable to me, but I can have no cause for complaint; only a few wistful regrets that I once spurned what I could have found in youth had I been less austere and sin conscious. As the psychiatrist also told me, the first half of my life was much too conditioned by oughts and ought nots.

Although my seventies were a decade of discoveries I found no room for complacency. One revelation is apt to be no more than a signpost to another, and by the time I turned eighty I'd found other avenues worthy of study and explanation. I could not for instance prove conclusively what I'd at times fondly believed was an extra portion of the feminine in my make-up. That each one of us has an element of the other sex in us, and that sex is not determined until the foetus is about six weeks old, is a fact beyond doubt. Variations from person to person of that element is highly probable simply because there is evidence of it from the mannish female to the effeminate male one encounters in any wide cross section of people. I would refute very strongly that I am effeminate, a trait which emerges in mannerisms and activities as if those affected have been endowed with less than one hundred per cent masculinity. I prefer to think that my male dosage was a hundred per cent but that the feminine endowment was additional in view of my works record. That widely misused term fetishism might be operative in my case but I have not fostered the idea. Nor is there proof. And not even supposition changes the basic fact that my eccentricity is an integral part of my nature. All my earnest attempts to deny or suppress it have miserably failed.

My first attempts at dismissal were out of fear. An impressionable, impulsive, imaginative nature is a seed bed for fear and guilt. Coupled with wanting to be good and liked by other people, especially adults, made for both ecstasies and agonies during my childhood. It led as I became older, as I've recorded, to obsessional activities and blunders as well as successes, but throughout my life I could not entirely get away from the influence that established Christianity and the Bible had on me. Since joining the Quakers I have become much more of a free thinker and more critical, but have remained a seeker.

As time runs out I have become more centred upon what might be ahead in the belief that one must always look forward if life has a purpose. To learn and perhaps benefit from past errors is all very well, but if life is seen as a progression in a religious or spiritual rather than the material sense, then there should be new perspectives as old ones fade away with the passage of time and circumstance. With shame I must admit that a lifelong fear of death remains with me. I tell myself that having had several years above the average I should be more willing to let go of life in preparation for death. But I keep up to the physical limitations which age imposes, even though I know I'm as dispensable as everyone else has to be. Nor can I yet believe wholeheartedly that there is an after life. I can but see this as possible because of so many of the discoveries — from computers to satellite communication — which would have been scoffed at as quite impossible eighty years ago, to say nothing of ESP.

Reincarnation appeals to me more than resurrection if there is an after life. It not only makes more sense to my way of thinking, but is perhaps more in keeping with the overall evolutionary principle. Nowadays I try to keep an open mind, to cut short imaginary conjecturings with the thought that it makes no difference because "Wait and see" is all that need be said. What matters much more is to be prepared to leave this life whether at a moment's notice or in a slow decline. A lot of unfinished business in the mind is bound to make transition or extinction, whichever it is, harder for ourselves and others we leave to follow on.

I spend several hours alone most days working with plants, propagating in one way or another. As with most repetitive work, familiarity allows thoughts to wander and very often I find mine going back to people I have known with mental pictures as they appeared seventy or more years ago. But if I'm having to work fast then one of the hymns I came to know by heart comes in both words and tune until the monotony makes me critical enough to employ my mind more usefully. But objective thinking on life's enigmas is beyond my ability. Other than on paper I cannot sustain a given subject, but a new thought occasionally comes out of the blue. And sometimes, when sleep is elusive, a kaleidoscope of portraits in colour comes one after the other of faces I have never seen before, complete with expressions and other details which make the procession quite interesting. And when sleep has almost come I still sometimes feel I am on a vast stretch of smooth ice, skating effortlessly at thirty miles an hour or more.

Having, as I hopefully believe, come to terms with myself at long last, such fantasies have taken the place of those more linked to my eccentricity. In times past I guess they were a kind of outlet or relief from tension, a kind of antidote to deprivation or lack of acceptance and understanding. But to try to rationalise the irrational is never likely to satisfy intellectually, and compromises are still needful not only in outward expression but inwardly as well in order to achieve a level-headed outlook and peace of mind. I have come to value this as coming from inner harmony and as a gift so great that it needs to be expressed by good will in any form towards others, regardless of who they are. Self-centred peace of mind is liable to be dangerous complacency, easily shattered by some unexpected event or situation. True peace of mind comes not only from the results of self knowledge and acceptance, with good will flowing. It comes also from seeking peace with humility and with pride strictly in its proper place. But pride can be insidious and I must take care not to take a pride in practising humility.

The saying "Pride comes before a fall" does not say it all. Some forms of pride for some people become so girded with the armour of prejudice as to make them immune to humiliation. On the other hand, there are those who have few pretensions, who see no virtue in being proud. They are apt to be trusting and therefore liable to be hurt far more when someone takes advantage of them by some manipulation. Rather oddly I have in the past been accused of manipulating others, yet have known occasions when I've been used, and to my shame and very much to my cost have quite recently been taken in. There's a fine line between humility and the gullibility which goes with a basically unsuspicious nature. But if the result of being hurtfully manipulated has to reduce what pride I took in any knowledge and judgment of human nature, the resultant humiliation has been a salutory lesson I needed to learn — the hard way again.

To become "as wise as serpents and as harmless as doves" is an ideal worth striving for. Such a state of mind is likely to bring peace of mind as the ideal way to live and mix in with others. But much as I've valued peace of mind at times when it has followed weariness and stress, I've always been somewhat afraid of becoming complacent. This fear began when as a regular churchgoer one of the regulation prayers spoken by the priest ended with "that we may pass our time in rest and quietness". As a teenage choirboy this was contrary to my view of life and its activities and so it has remained ever since. Living should surely be more adventurous than to exist complacently in rest and quietness. We are all, if healthy, gifted with minds and bodies which are meant to be used. How we use them is a matter of personal choice, but the potential and scope is always present, little or much, largely according to the amount of imagination we employ, as a prelude to incentive and action. It is better to try and fail than never to try to live fully.

Gain is often to be found in failure if we choose to profit by our mistakes. I believe that my many failures — wrong turnings, blunders, false notions — have enabled me to attain a measure of humility. I do not remember ever feeling complacent and self-satisfied. I can in no way set myself up as a paragon for having made achievements in spite of adversities, if only because some of the latter I have brought upon myself through lack of wisdom, vision and sensibility. Because of this dubious record I've reached old age with much gratitude rather than complacency and pride, but with resolves still intact to live as adventurously and usefully as circumstances allow. I might become physically decrepit and incapable of any kind of useful work, but so long as my mind functions reasonably I can never become complacent.

Complacency is, however, a state of mind capable of being stretched or expanded. In this context I do not include acceptance as defined earlier. Acceptance of one's essential nature and of the effects for good or ill from past mistakes, increasing limitations, and above all the approaching shadow of death, are far from being conducive to a state of complacency. The one is positive, but the other which I fear and reject is negative, having but a bleak future, without hope, forgiveness or redemption.

Forgiveness is a two-way matter, but what matters most is to forgive regardless those who have caused us harm or hurt. It is possible to bear grudges or resentment and to feel so righteous and justified in the process that it brings a kind of satisfaction complacently accepted, and in some cases to feed upon it as a source of energy. But such a use of energy is destructive of both peace of mind and spiritual progress. Thankfully I've been able to act in the belief that no matter what resentment others may carry towards me, I hold none against anyone, by means of forgiveness in my heart towards them.

This might be seen as trite, but it does not close my mind to regrets for hurt I must have caused and it is much more difficult to forgive myself convincingly than to forgive others. Come to think of it, I've never been able to bear resentment towards anyone for long, and sometimes have been able to find excuses for the person or persons concerned. This was an easy alternative way of finding release from an unnecessary, hampering burden, and with the advancing years it has formed part of the process of letting go of life's trammels and unhelpful prejudices.

In some aspects of life, however, I find it so far almost impossible to let go. The prospect of vegetating appals me, but I realise that sooner or later I will have to give up work which I am still able to enjoy. I enjoy using my body on manual work, hoeing, digging, planting, plant propagation during daylight hours, and in writing after the day's outdoor work is done. Outdoor work is healthful to body and mind and writing more often than not provides mental stimulation and a means of keeping in touch with others and with nature.

I have no illusions left of being indispensable. My job with plants is important and I can think of no one else capable of replacing me. But no doubt someone will be found when the time comes and until then I intend to carry on. What must be a much more important aspect of letting go is to be rid of non-essentials. This includes searching for answers to the teasing conundrums of life — to find the basic truths behind human existence, to seek assurance and a faith that will not shrink, or an unshakeable belief and trust in God. I can but suppose that I have made some spiritual progress in life. I've read lots of books but have spent very little time in prayer and perhaps if I'd done less of the former and more of the latter I would have made more progress spiritually. And now I believe it is time to let go of what no longer matters which clutters my mind and reduces its ability to see clearly what really does matter.

In coming to terms with myself, with trials and errors assisting self knowledge, I can feel a surer peace and, more important, more love seeping in. Self-knowledge encourages the necessary element of self-love which can then spread out pervadingly. My hopes rest on that love becoming ever stronger to reach its nadir with the acceptance of death as a new beginning.

Remorse, I've concluded, is another emotion which, like its opposite, resentment, has a clogging effect on both peace of mind and on learning to live progressively. It is a negative emotion when nothing can be done to remedy the cause, as when someone dies whom we are conscious of having wronged or neglected. I was inclined to harbour remorse after my father died for not having stayed at his bedside more than about half an hour, when there were signs enough that his end was not far off. The fact was that I deluded myself in a cowardly way instead of giving myself caringly to him when he needed me most. When I hinted that I could not stay, with lame excuses, he held out a hand and whispered, "Goodbye, old chap — I won't see you again." This brought a lump to my throat but still I could not let go, and although he lasted two more days, my thoughts and regrets might or might not have bridged the eighty miles distance between us at the time.

But somehow time has done so. Now that I have passed his then age, the fact that it would have been in his nature not to hold my neglect against me has helped me not to be burdened with remorse, and though I have never ceased to regret, the bond of love has strengthened over the years since 1957. And I am often reminded that he too enjoyed manual work. It was his decision at eighty-five to cut back a high thorn hedge overshadowing his garden that proved too hard a task. In laying up to recover from strain, other symptoms took hold and finally pneumonia prevailed.

I feel some sense of relief at having for the first time recorded this brush with remorse. In a peculiar way it is helpful in facing up to the Reaper, who before long will be knocking at my door — though he might not be so polite as this. Till recently, I have tended to take a more stoical attitude to the prospect of death — to go under fighting to the last breath within me. But this I now believe is not the way. A better way came through reading Damaris Parker-Rhodes' book, the title of which, The Way Out is the Way In, speaks for itself. This redoubtable Quaker lady came through many trials and tribulations before writing her book when she was aware that terminal cancer would cut short her life. She stressed the need for acceptance as have others who have come to terms with living in the shadow of impending death. Such examples give those of us without afflictions all the more cogent reasons for using what time remains to us in some worthy or worthwhile purpose.

Such thoughts began to niggle me about ten years ago when I was in my mid-seventies. My chosen form of retirement of working with plants and establishing the steam museum had included the added interest of six lecturing trips to America and Canada in the space of five years. It was stimulating until a reluctance to travel set in, and several new friendships were made. I felt an uneasiness of mind because it then seemed I had little else to do with the rest of my life other than to become fully engrossed in my work. The garden and its plants alone, I told myself, should have been satisfying enough. This and the now firmly established museum was bringing up to 150,000 visitors each year. Being an engine driver on the nursery railway added great pleasure and variety. Domestic life had become more tolerable, and since 1973 I'd had the privacy of my study with its bed to drop into at night. It was not ideal for either Flora or me, but it was a reasonable compromise, apart from the uneasiness which would not stop nagging my mind whenever I tried to peer into the future.

Three inhabitants in an eighteen-roomed house with one person elderly and out of tune with the other two seemed to make the empty rooms cry out for occupants. I was the only one to hear such calls but, because the household arrangements were not my province, my preferences had to be shelved. However, it was there on my mind and when, on separate occasions, some garden visitors each remarked on the therapeutic value of the garden to some people in need of relief from stress, this became a new perspective which I could not dismiss. Indeed, the more thought I gave to it the more it appealed to me. Here I was engrossed in my work, which seemed a worthwhile job in itself, but out there somewhere or other were people who could probably be helped over some acute, stressful problem, such as bereavement or the trauma of a broken marriage, by coming to stay long enough to find relief. I'd been so fortunate in being able to accumulate and display a very wide variety of perennials, and there were also the attractions for some in the relics of the steam age. For nature lovers there was the lake and the wilder parts of the fen and woods.

The house was central to all this, and I felt an increasing urge to share what I'd been able to bring about in the belief that such sharing, as on Open Days, was in a sense the fulfilment of my obsessional undertakings. To offer people in need of respite or renewal of interest in life the chance to share my home as guests at a modest charge would, I felt convinced, also provide an interest to the tail end of my life consistent with living fully and adventurously, so long as my selfish motives took second place. I couldn't kid myself that it was an entirely altruistic concept, if only because I saw that the status quo within my home was far removed from living fully.

I have no wish to dramatise this part of my story, because the snags and problems of going ahead with the idea were centred much more on people than on things. That my personal finances and assets were very slender was insignificant compared with the effect of the probable family disruption. Flora had played a central role as matron to the family, but would certainly not agree to keep house for strangers. She had often said her preference was for a much smaller house, but I had always refused to move away from where my vital interests and continuing work were. She had also been looking forward to retiring from her part-time job in the retail mail order section of the nursery. This she did very well, dealing with queries and the few complaints there were amongst the 35,000 yearly retail orders. What I failed to understand was her desire to have done with such responsibilities, but it was not for me to attempt to influence her whilst I built up my own resolve to take on an extra involvement. I had taken three years or more to reach a firm decision, knowing it would have to be irrevocable. Time was not on my side.

My eightieth year brought a request from the company's financial advisor to make over almost all my shareholdings to my sons. This was partly to avoid the possible adverse effect of estate duty at my death now that the firm had become one of the largest and most comprehensive nurseries in Britain. Adrian's efforts abroad had also brought international repute. One factor I found quite disturbing was that as both turnover and reputation soared, so profit margins diminished. Gold Medals for Chelsea Show exhibits did not guarantee financial stability and I'd always maintained that nursery stocks, being so perishable, were a liability until sold. A flood in late August 1987 brought some proof of this when over 100,000 ready-for-sale plants were rendered valueless. I spent that Bank Holiday weekend digging little trenches to save a 50,000 planting of new Crocosmias. And a few weeks later came the great gale which floored some 250 trees. A few were mature oaks, but most of them were poplars which I'd planted as windbreaks thirty years before!

It was just before these happenings that I first heard the term "Centre of Excellence" as a possible purpose to which my house could be put after my demise. I rather think it came first from the sales manager, but I rebelled inwardly once it came to my ears. I already knew that none of my family would wish to take it on as a residence — my sons having houses of their own. Being spacious and well placed the house could become, I was told, a kind of emblem or focus in keeping with the importance of the business with a library, conference and display rooms. The idea held no appeal whatever for me, alive or dead. It was too grandiose in my view and served only to foster my belief that it was the kind of house that needed to be lived in, if not by any of my descendants, then by people needing to stay for respite or recuperation. Even to merely offer B & B to visitors would be far more practical than the somewhat unrealistic, high falutin "Centre of Excellence". My proposal of only B & B could be quite rewarding in financial terms with so many visitors coming from a distance for the gardens, museum and sales centre. By 1989 I could no longer keep silent on what would likely be a family upheaval.

As expected, Flora refused to consider any part of my scheme and set about finding the kind of cottage she'd long wished to live in. Six months later she took what furniture and whatnot she needed — some being hers anyway. Having stayed with friends in Diss for two days during this process I came back to face the realities alone. It was a strange experience to walk from room to room; to be the sole occupant if only for a time. Flora not being obliged to be the sole occupant of her cottage two miles away, saved me from being conscious smitten, and rancour was absent on both sides. It was now up to me to put my somewhat hazy notions to the test of reality, with the feeling that I'd been stripped of both tensions and pretences.

From now on for the foreseeable future I was entirely responsible for the house, and my new freedom in solitude for a while would still be demanding. It had its price, not least the need to prove the genuineness of my aims and the purpose behind the drastic step I'd taken. Joan, who worked four days a week as a part-time helper-cum-cook had already agreed to stay on, for which I was truly thankful, especially as she had seventeen years of loyal, efficient service to her credit. Her co-operation was more vital than I'd ever imagined in the light of subsequent events.

Life's Jigsaw

Despite the relief of having the house to myself, after years of frequent tension with a break as the only acceptable solution, I was well aware that loneliness might well become intolerable. I placed an advertisement for a competent resident housekeeper. It was carefully worded to intimate that it was not to become a money-making guest house but to cater for people in need of respite and recuperation from stress. Inwardly, I hoped that it would appeal to a woman who had perhaps herself come through a rough time, who needed a home and a worthwhile job in congenial surroundings.

Several letters arrived, but very few replies appeared to be what I had in mind — I had an underlying hope of gaining a companion, much as I tried to convince myself that this was a very secondary consideration. After much sifting and several phone calls, two interviews took place with ladies who had to stay overnight due to the distance they had travelled. Both left never to be seen again. One asked for a salary I could not reach; the other had obvious attributes which to me were rather repellent. With that, after a month on my own, I could but renew the advertisement in *The Lady* and wait two more weeks for it to appear.

I got very few replies, and none were at all hopeful, but they coincided with another advertisement in the local press for someone to take charge of the steam roundabout. This had been a gift from me to Flora in 1967, but the Museum had bought it from her. And it was for this job that Angela applied, having just arrived from her native California for the second time in hopes of settling in England, with a love for East Anglia and a preference for its native males. The quickly arranged interview revealed that at forty she'd had three divorces but no children; could not be parted from her three Scotty terriers; was fully capable of running a household; had also an attraction for roundabouts and she badly needed a homely, settled life. The dogs, Angela told me, were waiting to be rescued from quarantine and she was in temporary accommodation not far from Bressingham; and so long as I would give the dogs a home, she was ready to take up whatever duties I wished, including redecorating a long since disused bedroom she'd noticed when I showed her around. Believing I was in luck, I made her welcome and overcame a dislike of yapping terriers by making a pen and what went for a kennel not far from the back door.

For the first few evenings we chatted when work was done, and found that we had similar tastes in music and literature as well as having much the same approach to spiritual matters. She longed, she said, for a settled life, but after a few days surprised me by announcing that she had a deep fascination for men. To a degree the statement intrigued me for she had an imposing Junoesque stature well above the average male, topping my 5ft 11ins. Being just about old enough to be her grandfather I assumed I was outside her imaginative sphere and felt it safe to respond to the "goodnight" peck she gave me after about a week.

Letters began to arrive for her and she told me that they were answers to an advertisement she'd put in the Personal Column of the *Eastern Daily Press*. She appeared to regard it as rather a joke and even invited me to read a few letters which she'd pursued with amused disdain. But from then on Angela went out most evenings leaving me to guess the reason and saying she'd be back by ten p.m. She seldom ever was, and one night phoned at past midnight to say that her car lights had failed and she was returning dead slow via back roads at little more than walking pace. After arriving safely at two a.m. she promised to be more considerate in future but reaffirmed her deep concern for her independence. In the lighter April evenings she helped me with kitchen garden jobs, always chatty and cheerful, as if she enjoyed the work and my company. My faithful daily help Joan hinted that Angela puzzled her but she could find no real cause for complaint in her work. I too was puzzled for there were contradictions in her behaviour and attitude to me. All I could think was that, after her somewhat turbulent life, it was taking her time to settle, and she gave no hints that any of the men she'd contacted through letters had appealed to her. This left me wondering where I stood, for there seemed ample evidence that she was content to stay on as resident housekeeper, though neither I nor anyone else took kindly to her noisy dogs.

On the third Sunday after Angela's arrival, I was working in the garden and she was indoors tidying her bedroom waiting for a lady friend to visit her.

At about four p.m. I heard the slam of a car door. Believing it signalled the friend's arrival I carried on with the intention of joining them for tea at half past four but, to my consternation, neither the friend's car nor Angela's were to be seen and the dogs too had gone. I went up to her bedroom and there found a note saying that she had to leave without telling me for fear I might persuade her to stay on. That fear was expressed a little more fully when she telephoned next day and gave the strong impression of her having feelings for me of which I'd been unaware. Perhaps I would have guessed had I been able to look into her eyes, but I never could because her fringe of hair obscured my view though obviously not her own vision.

If there was a lesson to be learned from this three-week episode I was in no mood to learn it. I felt badly let down. So much so as to welcome the relief of a belated enquiry from someone else who also lived not far away and was willing to come for an interview on learning that the position was unfilled. I was struck by her smart appearance as she stepped out of her car with an engaging smile.

"I'm Lilian," she announced, "and I know you're Alan Bloom because I've been here before and seen you driving a train, but I didn't like to speak to you."

Had she done so I might well have remembered her, for she too was well built with a comely face topped with curly blonde hair, and dangly earrings. She was quietly spoken and asked sensible questions as I showed her round the house and then the garden. Yes, she loved flowers and loved gardening as a change from cooking and housework. Her vivacity as well as her good looks quite impressed me. But when she told me that she'd been very ill, had suffered much bereavement and that she was divorcing her bad-tempered second husband and badly needed a congenial job, I could hesitate no longer. I was so convinced and impressed that I gave her the choice of bedrooms.

Lilian brought a car load of her own possessions a few days later — easy chairs, television, cushions, etc. as well as suitcases. And she brought her black retriever, having assured me that she was very docile and was no threat to the one cat I had. After making the bedroom cosy she requested the use of an extra cupboard to take the overflow of her clothes. Then with a smile of contentment, she asked what she could cook for my supper. That night I went to my bed-sitter feeling at last that my fortunes in the domestic sphere had taken a definite turn for the better.

The lady counseller whose name Lilian had given me as referee had been quite fulsome about her, based on interviews she'd had with her some months before. Added to this was Lilian's enthusiasm for my plan to take in guests in need, coupled with her expertise as a cook and her love of flowers and gardening. She assured me she had no personal axe to grind and she was a Christian. I was in no mood or position either to question or to disbelieve any of these assurances, but after a week or two I became aware of a puzzling physical attraction towards her. I was eighty-three and she was forty-three, but I became unsure of my expected immunity from that kind of involvement. It was, none the less, intriguing enough to find out how she felt about it. Lack of subtlety on my part in dealing with women on that level went with a lifelong tendency to be somewhat gullible in believing what people told me. It was not that Lilian said anything or even hinted, but just her manner, her very effective way of clothing and adorning her sumptuous body, and her good looks along with her merry laugh.

Sometimes in the evenings we took walks into the garden and around the lake, though nothing would induce her to go in my punt. One evening when we had almost circled the little lake, Lilian was unusually silent. Curious to know what might be on her mind I made a calculated remark which brought a swift unequivocal reply. "If you're referring to sex," she said with a pause, "I prefer a hot water bottle in bed with me. Much easier to deal with." I didn't think I'd been crude but said I was sorry if I had for I'd no wish to embarrass her. "I'll forgive you," she smiled, throwing a stick for her dog to run for. "You're not the only man who's jumped to the wrong conclusion — so don't you get any silly ideas."

About two weeks later Lilian became very concerned for her widowed stepmother. The old lady had suffered a heart attack and, although she'd been discharged from hospital, she needed somewhere she could more fully recuperate. "I feel it's my duty — and I'm quite fond of the old dear. So is it okay if I arrange for her to come here for a week or two? I promise I won't neglect my job."

With only a sprinkling of paying guests at the time — mostly for B & B — I agreed without hesitation and Lilian, having made arrangements by phone to fetch the old lady, then told me she would have to sleep downstairs. This seemed sensible, but when I asked which downstairs room she had in mind, she gave me an appealing smile and said she'd not asked me because she felt so sure I would agree to vacate the bed in my study just for a week or two. Taken aback, I blinked because I'd slept in it for nearly twenty years. "Just for a week or two," she pleaded, "and there's room in my bed for you. It's inevitable isn't it? The way I feel about you and how I guess you feel about me."

The stepmother said she was more than ready to return to her own house in less than the two weeks and Lilian gave me no encouragement to return to my own bed when she'd gone. After all, she said, she had lost her preference for a hot water bottle and was in fact more in love with me than with any man she had ever known. For me it was an experience so distinctive as to engender considerable reciprocity and when, by degrees, she brought up the possibility and advantage of marriage, this too fell into the category of inevitability, even though I was not free in that respect.

That my family were becoming alienated was increasingly evident and when I refused to announce publicly our intention to marry, she began ragefully to clear her dressing table as an indication of her intentions. After a somewhat traumatic hour, compromise was reached, but my uneasiness remained. It reached its peak when Jenny, my youngest daughter, braved Lilian's vitriolic tongue to plead with me. Then, and not till then, did it dawn on me how very unaware I'd been of my vulnerable position; and how far I'd allowed my judgment to be overruled. I could also see how the title of wife and mistress had appealed to her — enough to encourage her to go over the top in her efforts to achieve it. But my own feelings of shame tended to find excuses for her.

Lilian was having her day off with her daughter when I came to my senses. She telephoned to say that she would not be back till morning, and it was then that I told her I would be back in my own bed regularly. She made only enough comment to alert me of the confrontation to come. When she arrived, she set about silently emptying the dishwasher whilst I finished my breakfast at the kitchen table. She came round to my side of the table as if to replace the two mugs she held in her right hand. She stepped over her dog who, as usual, had flopped down where there was little or no room to avoid her. I stood up from the table and made room for Lilian to pass. Her eyes were blazing but I was not prepared for the two mugs which at less than arm's length hit my face close to my left eye. Somewhat dazed I made no response to her "Take that!"

Then she disappeared but came back a little later as I was putting on my boots near the back door. Standing on one leg I was not prepared for the swipe to my neck. It floored me and as I got up she disappeared again with a disdainful look of satisfaction on her face. Being somewhat bemused as I finished putting on my boots, I was not conscious of either anger or humiliation. It was a totally new experience for me, but strangely perhaps I had no thoughts of retaliation and could even feel sorry for her. She had realised that her spell over me was broken and her fond hopes had been shattered. Her resort to violence had in turn brought about my release in no uncertain way, removing at a stroke, literally, all the hostility she had created between me and my family. Yet it left me with a spontaneous willingness to forgive her. Even if she expressed no regrets for having lost her temper, I felt unwilling to give her immediate notice to leave. I felt it was up to her to say whether or not she wished to do so.

No reference was made all day to the early morning upset, but late that evening she said she would like to stay on and do the job she came for. I told her she could, but strictly on that basis. Apart from wishing to give her another chance, I had to take account of the increasing demand for B & B guests now that very few longer-stay people were booked to come, mainly because of Lilian's critical attitude towards them. Over the next few weeks an uneasy peace prevailed as the distance between us widened. Neither her petty complaints nor her tales, which centred on what appeared to be a wide circle of platonic friendships with men, registered deeply with me. I continued to hope that she would give me notice, but finally after about six weeks I had to do so formally and in writing to keep within the law. It coincided with the arrival of a man she'd invited for the weekend instead, as was more usual, of her going away. She took him up to her room with no introduction and there they stayed with door bolted and curtains drawn until he slinked away on the Monday morning. Lilian came down now and then for victuals saying that her friend had dire personality trouble and needed her full attention.

When I handed her the notice, she gave me the coldest of looks and accused me of acting through jealousy, adding that she preferred not to stay a day longer than needed to pack, and would employ a lawyer to see that she got every penny due for not working out a month's notice. I decided it was no time to argue, but was aware of her rising and indeed menacing temper. Joan heard her threatening voice, for she had been the first to know of her earlier violence. With commendable haste she went for the office telephone and asked my son Robert to come at once. I met him on the way and he phoned a solicitor for advice on his portable phone.

The next few days were quite hectic. I kept out of Lilian's way as she took the first car load of her belongings. A few days later she came back without warning and having found the door locked — a then regular precaution — she flew into a rage and grabbed a brick as if to throw it at a window, saying she had right of entry to get the rest of her belongings. It was her husband — whom she'd said she was divorcing — who restrained her. According to plan, I'd alerted a helper to be on call, and with his protection I let her in. I had been touched and grateful to others who had feared for my safety and, even if I was not really scared of a night time encounter, I was glad a Yale lock had been put on my bed-sitter door.

With that rather stressful week over, although intensely relieved, I was in quite a predicament because several guests were booked to arrive the day after Lilian finally left. I'd foreseen the need of a replacement and had advertised once more, but only one of the few answers offered sufficient promise to fix up an interview. To my further relief this one lady agreed to come open-endedly, but she explained that, being well into her sixties and having a heart condition, she could make no promises of being more than a temporary stop gap, although she was willing to come right away.

Ethel settled in quickly and good humouredly and gave me a renewed hope and confidence. I'd had no time to ask for, much less take up references, and if most of her experience had been in responsible nursing positions, she had no problems in coping with B & Bs and housekeeping. She too was a divorcee, and had suffered hardships; and she seemed glad to have me as a listener to her past misfortunes and adventures. Ethel came in mid-September and was still coping when December came in, taking only a day or so off weekly to return to her flat thirty miles away. In my new feeling of contentment, I could overlook her occasional lapses into mild extravagence with food, new bedroom equipment and heating as winter set in.

This forgivable fault occurred especially when Ethel prepared for Christmas. Three guests were due to come for a week over the holiday — two being elderly women friends of her's, and a younger woman recommended by her therapist, who had seen an article I wrote for the *Friend* weekly. Ethel insisted on a well-decorated Christmas tree and other festive displays but not, I was glad to note, some mistletoe as I'd never been one to enjoy casual or compulsory kissing, and I was the only male there. The two elderly friends duly arrived at

Diss station and Ethel fetched them in her own car. One, with the surname Sheridan, spoke with obvious authority over the other who had a decidedly foreign accent. The disparity intrigued me and when later I enquired the origin of her name, she said it was too complicated to explain.

Janet, who came in her own car from Huntingdon, was very different as well as being younger, and was far less self-assured than Ms Sheridan. Her features betrayed much suffering and she admitted that her agrophobia had made her coming at all very difficult.

Never before had I been in such a position or environment to help someone in need of sympathy, understanding and help. I was not aware of any gifts in that direction, although I had been conscious of wanting to help with the aid of the garden which, as I have already explained, was my main objective in opening my house to guests in need. During the first year I had tried to get through to two or three such guests but had failed to make any real impact; partly, no doubt, to the negative effect of Lilian's influence. But during the first conversation with Janet I was aware of an upsurge of feeling along with a growing belief that here was someone who not only needed the kind of help I wished to give, but who would respond wholeheartedly to gentle, unalloyed encouragement. Something strangely reciprocal and mutually beneficial had clicked between us. My being much the age of her recently deceased father, with whom she had felt emotional security had, we decided, some important bearing on the mutual trust which had emerged so soon after our first talk together.

As I write this four years later Janet is still here. With similar tastes in most aspects of life we soon became companionable. She enjoys working with me and can switch from serious conversation to indulging in our somewhat zany or goonish sense of humour. Her leanings towards Bhuddism are not far from my own Quaker ways of thought and, if her progress towards freedom from the depression, which has for so long marred her life, has been slow she has come a long way since Christmas 1990 with her feet now firmly on the road forward. And all along I have been aware of a kind of blessing descending on me for what little cost it has been to me in terms of giving the kind of help she needed. I know now that I needed to be able to give such help — and from letters received from a few other women who have stayed during the past year or two, there seems to be some proof of an ability, without conceit and without consciously trying, to be helpful to others.

I would welcome, provisionally, an opportunity to learn if I could be of similar help to a man, but must admit to a preference for women in this context. With age I have become aware of an empathy towards women I never felt when younger. This could be put down to ignorance and indoctrination which led to a bedevilling ambivalence causing hurt and unhappiness which I still regret. Envy, fear, admiration and domination used to taunt me in turn and it was not until I came to understand my own peculiar make-up that I began to understand women's. I would like to believe that, despite the conflicts of one kind and another both with women and within myself, there is a link with my present attitude towards them. In other words, that some feminine element in my genes has at last found a deeper, truer means of expression.

The relief for me in having no resident housekeeper, after trying several more when Ethel had finally departed, was in sharp contrast to the earlier belief that one was vital for my new venture. Perhaps it will still prove to be a necessity, but in the event the guests who have stayed since then have been well enough cared for by part-time helpers to leave some very appreciative remarks in the visitors' book.

Discoveries

Bill — the man who wanted to know what made me tick — might or might not be enlightened if he reads this book. Having written it, exposing myself in the process to some extent, I have a feeling that by this means I have come to better understand not only myself, but women too. Since I reached seventy I have become less mentally cluttered and less influenced by earlier ambitions, indoctrinations, with a freedom of mind which has continued to expand, especially in the past three to four years. Although some of the women I came to know rather well were less than admirable in my view, they might well say the same of me. But for my edification, Janet has been quite outstanding for her complete honesty, and her sheer goodness of heart has been a blessing indeed to me, as well as her being a companion with whom I feel completely at ease.

These encounters and experiences have helped me, not only to understand and appreciate women in a more general way, but to rationalise the feminine element within myself. I can imagine very few men would be aware of, or care to admit to, the existence of any feminine element in their make-up. Nor would many women encourage them to do so, and much less to foster it, when for centuries men have regarded women as the second sex, made by God, to serve them and rear their offspring. The term "opposite sex" has jarred on me in the belief that the two are, or should be, fully complementary, as they are in the rest of the animal world. Sex equality, however, is another false ideal and women who shout for it are in the wrong, because it sets up harmful competition to the true ideal of sharing the responsibilities of life in harmony.

It is only during the twentieth century that positive but halting attempts to undo the harm which thousands of years of women's subjection to men have begun, and only in the more prosperous parts of the world. And that most cruel and shameful practice of female circumcision is still practised widely in some areas as a means of degradation. Cruelty, however, is one of the many expressions of the human free choice of good or evil. Nor is its practice confined to men, for history has some examples of women with mercilessly cruel natures. Cruelty is, of course, one aspect of the corruption that comes from power, just as lust for power is one of the main objectives of greed.

Aside from this, it seems indisputable that more tenderness lies in female attributes, and even if this is part of the child-bearing role, its expression goes beyond that role. This is no more than a generalisation. Most men's reluctance to see any part of their make-up or psyche as being feminine is, no doubt, the reason why the subject is so seldom brought up for discussion or explanation. It has in fact been used in the popular press as a veiled or amusing slur on the character of a few men in the public eye.

It would be foolish of me to extol feminine qualities as being superior to those of men. Both sexes have the propensity for good and evil, stemming from the inherited power of imagination, along with the choice or ability to put conscious or deliberate thought into action. But over thousands of years of male domination, women have naturally and understandably developed their own techniques in order to survive, or at least to hold their own with childbearing a handicap in the physical sense. Although childbearing was and still is a form of creativity, the latter also found a further outlet as women were probably the first cultivators, essentially for food. With civilisation, subjugation by men led to the underlying battle of the sexes — women's wiles against men's muscles.

If indeed the "female is deadlier than the male", then this is probably the result of male domination over many centuries. What I have often puzzled over is the reason why, in certain respects, men appear to have been the more creative in the arts and especially in painting, sculpture and music. Although in literature women are catching up with men which comes from being allowed more education over the past two centuries, it is still difficult to account for discrepency in the other arts unless childbearing and lack of freedom have been the basic reason.

It would be interesting to read what an in-depth study might reveal on the subject of interaction between the sexes which, I fancy, is at the root of male creativity in its many forms and expressions. There is already very substantial evidence that males, as the second sex, are born with varying doses of female in their genetic make-up. It appears not so easy to account for the male element in women, though this was accepted in the ancient Chinese philosophy of Yin and Yang for thousands of years. It is also accepted by modern psychologists that the fusion of opposites within human psyches releases powerful energies which demand some outlet or expression. How such energy is applied depends upon the nature of a person, and to his or her attitude to good and evil.

Large numbers of each sex are in favour of the maximum distinction between the two. "Vive la différence" is still popular, but it does not alter the fact that some basic attributes are shared. It would seem beyond doubt that such variations are congenital, or one of the facts of life, even if some people show no signs and are not aware of it. In the present climate of opinion — or I might say the present stage of human social evolution — the vast majority of individuals would prefer to regard themselves as entirely male or female. Only a few have intimations of the other sex in their make-up, as I had at a very early age, and it took a very long time — almost a lifetime — to accept it for what it is.

What stands out is that, even if the vast majority of people believe themselves to be entirely masculine or feminine, everyone has something of the opposite sex in their genes and make-up. Having myself been aware from a very early age of this complexity, I can explain its effect on my life's work through my intimacy with the women with whom I had the closest contact. With hindsight, it is easy to see that ignorance and indoctrination backed by religion during my formative years would sooner or later collide with my somewhat thrusting, imaginative basic nature. For much of that time and until I married at twenty-four, fantasies were some outlet for inner conflicts and frustrations. Apart, of course, from the outlet provided by almost obsessively using pent up energies at work, play or whatever. At times I became somewhat reclusive, and one recurring and rather haunting fantasy was of living entirely alone in some remote place in Canada, pioneering or pitting my wits to survive in a harsh but natural environment.

Such notions were in complete opposition to those of a settled life in harmony with a perfect partner. This was the ideal, in the belief that in such a state I could find my true self, whilst carrying out my basic ambition to build up a substantial nursery business — to be ordinary, to be content.

The first years of marriage brought disillusionment but, apart from a somewhat cussed determination to do all in my power to shore up the shaky foundations by whatever means which offered hopes of stability, it was a duty not to be shirked. This, however, was hampered by desires of self expression, to find outlets for my energies outside the bonds of marriage. The need to spend more time and thought on my own, to make as it were distinct compartments, set alight a previously constrained imagination. The ideal of two persons becoming one, as the marriage service enjoined, was after all false and impractical. I was beginning to realise I'd made a monumental blunder and, even if I was willing and anxious to make the best of a bad job, my upsurging thoughts and feelings of a more selfish kind were too strong and demanding to be resisted entirely.

At this stage I was unable to stamp out the inklings of something feminine in my make-up. They were completely beyond my understanding; so much so that I could not imagine anyone else having them. It had to be my secret and I had to deny any expression of it which carried the slightest risk of exposure. It formed part of my growing obsession to use my energies worthily as a means of self expression, so to smother a secret trait which carried a shameful connotation and a guilty conscience.

The early 1930s were not conducive for starting up a new business with virtually no capital. But thanks to my parents' willingness to let me take over the Oakington property at a modest rent, its fifteen acres of fertile soil was almost ideal on which to begin a nursery. I had formed a few notions on principles on which such a business should flourish. These were proving to be sound by the time my ideals on marriage were being whittled away to be replaced with the search for wider and more ambitious outlets. Having always had to be quite frugal and careful with money in the past, expansion could only come out of profits. Standing by my exhibit at the Chelsea Show in 1934 was a turning point. The tedium of waiting for people's orders for plants became unbearable and I decided to become a mail order wholesaler.

It was this decision which allowed my imagination to open up because it gave me more time, not solely to produce plants for retailing nurserymen, but to become more creative in a modest way. I began to study hybridising to raise new varieties and to improve soil productivity along with effective irrigation and drainage. By 1936 I began to look for more land to compete with the Dutchmen, as well as to write articles for the horticultural press. And I was finding that amongst the increasing numbers of helpers were some who seemed to share my enthusiasms. Not all of my schemes were worthy or realistic and a few proved to be failures — such as making a pond with hand labour. Nor when I took on more land which proved to be unsuitable for one reason or another for what I had planted on it. I should perhaps have been more cautious when venturing on to Black Fen land in 1937. It was rented and twelve miles away. Within weeks of planting four acres and 120,000 plants, they were drowned in a spring flood. Yet in 1938 with an unexpected additional profit, I paid £1,600 for a 200-acre farm in the fens. This, and what it led on to, has already been described and it was the onset of war along with my marriage break-up which forced me to take stock of my complex motivations.

The first intimations that there was some underlying motive in my forceful attitude to life and work had come when I sought relief from the delusions of trying to be conventional, or normal, in the accepted sense. This was linked closely with doctrinal Christianity, but little by little most of those precepts proved invalid and only a friendship with a new vicar of my own age for a time avoided an end to church going. It was with very gradual acceptance that I saw my furious activity as a kind of substitution or sublimation which stilled to some extent my inner conflicts. Even so, I could only see this as a partial explanation — a case of alleviating painful frustrations by plunging into hectic activities. The enigma of my secret link with something feminine deep down within me remained a mystery. It only ceased to niggle me when I was up to my neck in some absorbing activity, and when in close contact with my three young children — lacking in a mother's loving care.

This lack appeared to have been filled with the arrival of Myrah in 1944. Within days I was convinced that she would become an ideal substitute mother and within a month this concept included my own need as well. Our respective needs appeared to have been met. But clashes came along with her painful silences which I could not break through. I lacked understanding of her situation, she lacked truthfulness, and yet we both imagined that by emigrating to Canada all our problems would vanish. It had the opposite effect, pushing each of us into ourselves and to a final parting in 1956 after twelve years.

I have recapped just to give a more intimate picture of my own waywardness. I can no longer feel shame for this because acceptance of my eccentricity has gradually brought much needed peace of mind. The road to understanding was hard and devious but, just as it would have been easier had I been born fifty years later, it could have ruined my life if fifty years sooner. Perhaps an upsurge of creativity as a sublimation, as seems likely in my own case, is alive in many others who have not had the means as I have of giving expression to it. There were times when no thought occurred of my being creative. The job in hand was too absorbing, ruling out also any materialistic motivation. For this I am thankful indeed, because what I have gained in peace and harmony, and appreciation expressed by visitors, is beyond price.

To reach old age with such a blessing in no way gives me cause for self satisfaction and complacency. Having to let go, to come to terms with death, entails much more than resignation to the inevitable. Dimly I have become aware of the vital need to concentrate my mind away from my earthly self or ego. If life has any meaning at all, it must surely be linked to some infinity in which the spiritual takes over from the material. If we try to hold on to the material side of life — which centres on the personal — then it must be hard, and perhaps impossible, to meet the radical change or transition from life as we have known it to the unknown beyond. To achieve this would seem to require a new and different phase or form of consciousness whilst we still have a choice to do so. But this is very difficult indeed.

A longing for peace and harmony have been much in my mind for several years. I see them as a need above almost all else and as being indivisible or complementary. But if for me they have proved to be rather transient or elusive, I have at least learned that even more valuable and more vital is the need to seek humbly the peace and harmony which comes from within. And needs be I must dismiss any lingering sense of grievance for having given away so much of what I worked hard to acquire. This now hampers my deep desire to form my house and garden into a Trust. I can but hope and strive that it will come about, even if I do not live long enough to see it.

I've now reached an age in which peace of mind and harmony are the most precious of all life's blessings. To count my blessings is much more conducive than to dwell upon my mistaken ideas and blunders. One of the greatest of my blessings in recent years has been the way in which my son-in-law, Jaime Blake — Anthea's husband — has taken on full responsibility for the garden. He had had virtually no experience or knowledge of plants and had qualified as a teacher, but in finding this was not his bent, drifted into park work at Peterborough. It was in getting to know him on visits to Bressingham, when I was looking out for help, that I had a hunch he had the basics of aptitude and devotion. And now, seven years later, I rank my decision to enlist him as one of the best I ever made. He has performed even beyond my highest hopes, so much so that he now sometimes comes up with suggestions which I can accept as improvements on those I first practised.

To achieve perfection in a garden of this size and complexity is, I've found, a will o' the wisp kind of ambition. This is the main reason why any pride of achievement has to take a back seat in my mind; and so it does to have the garden seen as a memorial to me as its creator. Without wishing to indulge in false modesty, I consider it more important to share what I have been fortunate enough to create, and to ensure such sharing shall continue well beyond my lifetime.

LARGE PRINT

ISIS publish a wide range of books in large print, from fiction to biography. A full list of titles is available free of charge from the address below. Alternatively, contact your local library for details of their collection of ISIS books.

Details of ISIS unabridged audio books are also available.

Any suggestions for books you would like to see in large print or audio are always welcome.

ISIS
7 Centremead
Osney Mead
Oxford OX2 0ES
(0865) 250333

BIOGRAPHY AND AUTOBIOGRAPHY

Winifred Beechey	**The Reluctant Samaritan**
Christabel Bielenberg	**The Road Ahead**
Kitty Black	**Upper Circle**
Navin Chawla	**Mother Teresa**
Phil Drabble	**A Voice in the Wilderness**
Daphne du Maurier	**The Rebecca Notebook and Other Stories**
Lady Fortescue	**Perfume From Provence**
Gillian Gill	**Agatha Christie**
Paul Heiney	**Farming Times**
Paul Heiney	**Second Crop**
Brian Hoey	**The New Royal Court**
Ilse, Countess von Bredow	
	Eels With Dill Sauce

BIOGRAPHY AND AUTOBIOGRAPHY

Paul James	**Margaret**
Paul James	**Princess Alexandra**
John Kerr	**Queen Victoria's Scottish Diaries**
Margaret Lane	**The Tale of Beatrix Potter**
Bernard Levin	**The Way We Live Now**
Margaret Lewis	**Ngaio Marsh**
Vera Lynn	**Unsung Heroines**
Peter Medawar	**Memoir of a Thinking Radish**
Michael Nicholson	**Natasha's Story**
Angela Patmore	**Marje**
Marjorie Quarton	**Saturday's Child**
Martyn Shallcross	**The Private World of Daphne Du Maurier**
Frank and Joan Shaw	**We Remember the Blitz**
Joyce Storey	**Our Joyce**
Douglas Sutherland	**Born Yesterday**
James Whitaker	**Diana v. Charles**

(A) Large Print books also available in Audio

GENERAL NON-FICTION

Eric Delderfield	**Eric Delderfield's Bumper Book of True Animal Stories**
Caroline Elliot	**The BBC Book of Royal Memories 1947-1990**
Joan Grant	**The Cuckoo on the Kettle**
Joan Grant	**The Owl on the Teapot**
Helene Hanff	**Letters From New York**
Martin Lloyd-Elliott	**City Ablaze**
Elizabeth Longford	**Royal Throne**
Joanna Lumley	**Forces Sweethearts**
Vera Lynn	**We'll Meet Again**
Desmond Morris	**The Animal Contract**
Anne Scott-James and Osbert Lancaster	**The Pleasure Garden**
Les Stocker	**The Hedgehog and Friends**
Elisabeth Svendsen	**Down Among the Donkeys**
Gloria Wood and Paul Thompson	**The Nineties**
The Lady Wardington	**Superhints for Gardeners**
Nicholas Witchell	**The Loch Ness Story**

WORLD WAR II

Paul Brickhill	**The Dam Busters**
Reinhold Eggers	**Escape From Colditz**
Fey von Hassell	**A Mother's War**
Dorothy Brewer Kerr	**The Girls Behind the Guns**
Vera Lynn	**We'll Meet Again** (A)
Vera Lynn	**Unsung Heroines**
Tom Quinn	**Sea War**
Frank and Joan Shaw	**We Remember the Battle of Britain**
Frank and Joan Shaw	**We Remember the Blitz**
Frank and Joan Shaw	**We Remember D-Day**
William Sparks	**The Last of the Cockleshell Heroes**
Anne Valery	**Talking About the War**

POETRY

**Long Remembered:
Narrative Poems**

INSPIRATIONAL

Thora Hird	**Thora Hird's Praise Be! Notebook**

REFERENCE AND DICTIONARIES

The Longman English Dictionary
The Longman Medical Dictionary

TRAVEL, ADVENTURE AND EXPLORATION

Jacques Cousteau	**The Silent World**
Peter Davies	**The Farms of Home**
Patrick Leigh Fermor	**Three Letters From the Andes**
Keath Fraser	**Worst Journeys**
John Hillaby	**Journey to the Gods**
Dervla Murphy	**The Ukimwi Road**
Freya Stark	**The Southern Gates of Arabia**
Tom Vernon	**Fat Man in Argentina**
A Wainwright	**Wainwright in the Limestone Dales**
Dylan Winter	**A Hack in the Borders**

(A) Large Print books also available in Audio